GOLGONOOZA *City of Imagination*

Golgonooza

LAST STUDIES IN

by

City of Imagination

WILLIAM BLAKE

KATHLEEN RAINE

GOLGONOOZA
PRESS

Published by Golgonooza Press
3 Cambridge Drive, Ipswich IP2 9EP, U.K.

British Library Cataloguing in Publication Data
Raine, Kathleen *1908–*
Golgonooza, city of imagination: last studies in William Blake.
1. Poetry in English. Blake, William, 1757–1827
I. Title
821.7

ISBN 0 903880 43 1 *cloth*
ISBN 0 903880 44 X *paper*

Typeset by Goodfellow & Egan, Cambridge
Printed by St Edmundsbury Press

To my co-founders of *Temenos* 1981–1991

Philip Sherrard   Keith Critchlow   Brian Keeble

I never made friends but by spiritual gifts,
By severe contentions of friendship & the burning fire of thought.
(Jerusalem 91 : 17–8)

Contents

Introduction

WHEN in the 1930s I first attempted to read Blake's Prophetic Books they were incomprehensible to me, altogether outside the terms of reference I had known hitherto in my reading of the mainstream of English poetry. Blake's visions of the inner events of England's national life seemed a phantasmagoria; in that bewildering mythological world, events and enactors belonged to a universe in which times and places were correspondences of states of being, rather than possessing even such location and duration and sequence within a stable world as Milton has established in *Paradise Lost*. My generation possessed no clue to this inner universe of ever-shifting symbol, to the identity or nature of the Four Zoas and their feminine emanations and other more transient enactors of some inner mood or event. Who were they? In what drama were they so vitally engaged? Yet so luminous are the *Songs of Innocence and Experience*, so sure the aim of the aphorisms of *The Marriage of Heaven and Hell* that I could not believe that Blake's insights into inner events of England's national life did not, when understood, contain meaning no less profound. No doubt it was a sense of the insufficiency of the then current modes of thought and critical criteria that unwove all rainbows that drew me to Blake, whose world was so totally beyond the scope of these measures. This was a world in which the current terms employed in our Universities for the discussion of literature were meaningless. Thus I began to wind Blake's 'Golden String' into a ball. The length of that string and its many windings astonished me then; the golden simplicity of the sphere that remains in my hands amazes me now.

In the academic world researchers talk of their 'subject', and often in both senses of the word – 'subject' not only as a field of study, but also as if the poet were himself 'subject' to their theories, often indeed 'subjected' to the Procrustean mutilation of some transient fashion. Poets read the same works but for other reasons, principally in search of meaning and wisdom. Blake has not been my 'subject' but my Master, in the Indian sense of the word. Little by little I came first to discern, and gradually to understand something of the nature and the extent of that wisdom. Blake challenged not merely some aspect or shortcoming in the intellectual, political and social world of his time – a time of revolution and war, the birth of America and the death of the old regime in France and Europe – but the very premisses of modern Western civilization, the very ground of Western materialism, already in his day displacing an older learning established in totally other premisses. In this battleground between incompatible ideologies it is to be noted that Blake's young disciples, the painters Palmer and Calvert and the rest, named themselves 'the Shoreham Ancients', indicating that their values were those of antiquity, as against 'the moderns' of science and 'progress'.

Materialism holds 'matter' (whatever that may be) to be the ground of reality; other civilizations, and the older culture of Europe also, have held the view that not matter but mind, spirit – not the observed but the observer – is that ground. In the course of my studies the paradigm of the world I had unthinkingly inherited was totally transformed. For W. B. Yeats too (who with the Pre-Raphaelite Edwin J. Ellis had been the first editor of Blake's Prophetic Books) Blake had been a Master and it was Yeats whose commentaries and interpretations put into my hand the clue I was to follow for the next twenty years – indeed for the rest of my life. I had at one time thought of making a study of Blake in terms of Jungian psychology; but while it is true that Jung's paradigm of the psyche may guide the seeker into that world at the outset, Blake goes as far beyond Jung as Dante travelled beyond Virgil, his first guide. Nor can Blake be understood as an example of the spontaneous manifestation of an archetypal structure common to all: the many similarities are to a great extent because having discerned that inner universe, both Blake and Jung discovered and pursued a tradition that relates to that order—a 'learning of the Imagination' that comprises an extensive tradition excluded from modern academic studies. They had read the same books—essentially the Platonic tradition, the Neoplatonists and the Hermetica, the Gnostics and the Alchemists, Boehme and Paracelsus and Swedenborg. Blake had discovered and given new life, at the end of the eighteenth century, to the hidden traces of the Perennial Philosophy, which, in the words of his one-time friend Thomas Taylor the Platonist, is 'coeval with the universe itself; and however its continuity may be broken by opposing systems, it will make its appearance at different periods of time, as long as the sun himself shall continue to illumine the world.' (*Eleusinian and Bacchic Mysteries*, Introduction) Blake's 'system' that to scholars trained in modern Western universities has often appeared obscure is in reality grounded in Plato and the pre-Socratics, Plotinus and the Neoplatonic succession, which through Ficino and the Florentine school continued to be, both outside and within Christianity, the mainstream of European civilization until superseded by the modern scientific school.

At this point I should perhaps say that the Traditional school of René Guénon, Coomaraswamy and their successors was brought to my notice at the time I was beginning my Blake studies by my friend Philip Sherrard, who himself belongs to that group. I found much of value in the writings of Guénon, and, more relevant to my own studies, those of Coomaraswamy, concerned as he was with the metaphysics of aesthetics and the arts, and who actually had the perspicacity to place Blake beside Dante himself as representing, within the European context, 'traditional' art. Two members of that group—Titus Burckhardt and Philip Sherrard himself—have made radical attacks on Jung and in so doing revealed the limitations of that school. 'Tradition', as understood by followers of Guénon, for all their insistence on 'revealed' knowledge and the metaphysical order, seems unconnected to the living source itself and highly suspicious of those very inner worlds from which it ultimately derives. That inner world both Blake and Jung affirm, and both appreciated the value of the alchemical symbolism and the alchemical 'work' of self-transformation. Blake praises Jacob Boehme above all other spiritual masters whom he had studied, and Boehme affirms that the seeker for God must find the living source within. I find what is missing from Guénon and his followers in the writings of Henry Corbin, who, together with Jung, was among the founding members of the Eranos circle, and whose term, the 'imaginal', describes the order to which Blake's Prophetic Books belong—as it does Jung's world of psyche and its archetypes. Corbin understands that sacred tradition is itself without meaning outside that context. His own studies are of the Ismaili Sufi tradition, one branch of the recorded history of humanity's experience of that world of inner reality. These realities cannot be known by mere subscription to a doctrine, but demand a certain level of spiritual development and practise; yet at the same time are universal realities accessible to all. Corbin thus harmonizes what one might call the Protestant vision of Blake and Jung, their insistence on discovering the truth 'within the human breast', and the recognition of a tradition of sacred knowledge embodied in every civilization and all mythologies.

Uncomprehended though he was, Blake was not, like Yeats, an esotericist. He addressed his prophetic message 'to the Public' and whether he would be understood he did not stop to question—his vision was, to him, clear beyond all doubt. He was a patriot of the inner worlds, of the England of the Imagination whose 'golden builders' he saw everywhere at work in the creation of Golgonooza, the city within the brain (*golgos*, skull), 'the spiritual fourfold

London eternal'. He saw his nation 'sunk in deadly sleep', victim of the 'deadly dreams' of a materialism whose effects in all aspects of national life were destructive and sorrowful, wars, exploitation of human labour, sexual hypocrisy, a 'cruel' morality of condemnation and punitive laws, the denial and oppression of the soul's winged life. To many of a younger generation Blake's writings, however partially understood, have become sacred books. And now that we have begun to disentangle his mythology, to know who the Four Zoas are and what their natures, how very familiar and English are these modern embodiments of undying moods—Urizen, 'aged Ignorance', blind reason with his heavy books of the law, forever striving to impose his narrow systems and to order the boundless creativity of life, clipping the wings of fiery youth; Vala in her 'garden' of nature, Jerusalem, the soul outcast like a 'beggar in the streets' of London; Los, spirit of Inspiration, creating and destroying, in his furnaces, with his blacksmith's hammer and anvil, the productions of Time. Who does not know God appearing to Job in his whirlwind, and the Creator setting his compasses to the deep? These archetypal figures seem as native to the English imagination as Hamlet and Lear and Prospero; they are not inventions but portraits of archetypes; they are ourselves.

To live by the Imagination is Blake's secret of life. The 'gods' of reason, feeling, inspiration and the physical senses, are but aspects of that single life of Imagination, 'the human existence itself' which embraces all in unity. There is nothing outside the Imagination, which is immortal, eternal, and boundless. The first *Life* of Blake, written by Thomas Gilchrist, was completed by William Michael Rossetti, brother of the poet-painter, and thus Blake came to influence the Pre-Raphaelite Brotherhood, and, through them, W. B. Yeats. But Blake's religion of the Imagination was by no means the 'art for art's sake' of the late nineteenth century. On the contrary, Blake roundly condemns as 'false art' all that is not inspired and informed by the Imagination, all mere copying of the appearances of things. On his engraving, made late in life, of the

Laocoön Group Blake inscribed his *credo* of the religion of the Imagination: 'The Eternal Body of Man is the Imagination, that is, God himself . . . It manifests itself in his Works of Art (In Eternity All is Vision)'. Blake is not the originator of the concept of the Imagination as the second Person of the Trinity: according to his own spiritual Master, Boehme, the Creation is 'the Imagination of God'. For Blake, therefore, the God within is 'Jesus, the Imagination', the Divine Humanity, present in all and to all men. 'The religion of Jesus', as Blake understood it, is the life of the Imagination; Jesus and his apostles and disciples were 'all artists'. In his Introduction to the fourth and last book of *Jerusalem*, 'To the Christians', Blake concludes with the exhortation, 'Let every Christian, as much as in him lies, engage himself openly & publicly before all the world in some Mental pursuit for the Building up of Jerusalem.'

In Eastern civilizations some form of meditation is the norm of spiritual practise. For Blake art was such a practise and the arts are the channels through which visions of these 'eternal things displayed' are embodied and disseminated. 'Prayer is the Study of Art. Praise is the Practise of Art'. Prayer is receptive, praise active: the one must precede the other. Blake's own reverence for the great works of all ages should remind us that there can be no practise without study. This has perhaps been forgotten somewhat in the nation-wide revolution in which the writing of verse has become the practise of multitudes – a revolution which can surely be traced through Herbert Read's 'education through art' to William Blake's call to the English nation to live the life of the Imagination, and the vision in which 'Everything that lives is Holy.' Imagination is the ladder on which angels forever ascend and descend.

The papers collected in this volume do not constitute a systematic study of Blake. In *Blake and Tradition* (Bollingen Series xxv:2, Princeton University Press, 1981) and in the shorter version (text of the Andrew Mellon Lectures given in that year) *Blake and*

Antiquity I uncovered some of Blake's sources relating his works to themes of the Platonic tradition, and in *The Human Face of God* Blake's Job engravings to symbolic terms and themes in his own writings. (Thames & Hudson, 1982). All the papers in this collection were written for some specific occasion; most are revised, to minimize repetition, and some extensively re-written.

'Science and Imagination in William Blake' was first delivered as a paper at a conference in Cordova organized by *France Culture* and was subsequently printed in *Temenos* 1, 1981: 'Blake and *Maya*' was first given as a paper in New Delhi at the India International Centre and later published in *Indian Horizons* Vol., XXXII, No.3, 1983: 'Mythologizing of Time in Blake's Prophetic Books' was given at a conference on Time organized by the Indira Gandhi National Centre for the Arts, New Delhi, November 1990, and is to be published in the Proceedings of that Conference: 'Blake, Swedenborg and the Divine Human' and 'The City in Blake's Prophetic Poetry', were given (in French) at l'Université St-Jean de Jerusalem (founded by Henry Corbin) in Paris and published in the *Cahiers* (numbers 9 and 12) of that Society: 'The City in Blake's Prophetic Poetry' was also given to the Newcastle Literary and Philosophic Society (1985): 'Suffering According to Blake's Illustrations of Job', a condensed version of my book *The Human Face of God*, 1982, was given as a paper to the Blake Society, St. James's, Piccadilly, London, 1983: 'The Apocalypse—Blake and Michelangelo' was delivered at the British Council, Rome: 'The Sleep of Albion' was first given at a Celtic conference at the University of Toronto, 1985, and at the Second Merlin Conference, London, 1987, and subsequently published in *Merlin and Woman*, Edited by R. J. Stewart, Blandford Press, 1988.

Science & Imagination in William Blake

William Blake is the only English poet whose central theme is the confrontation of science and imagination. To Blake the radical error of Western civilization lies in the separation, originating perhaps with Aristotle and now universally accepted within modern secular societies, between mind and its object, nature. Blake's inspired but uncomprehended message was neither more nor less than to declare and demonstrate the disastrous human consequences of this separation, and to call for a restoration of the original unity of being in which outer and inner worlds are one. By the end of the eighteenth century religion itself, in the form of Deism, 'natural religion', had ceased to question the definitions of space, time and matter elaborated by post-Cartesian science; had ceased to perceive that any alternative account of the natural universe could be seriously considered. Blake's questioning of these premisses – insofar as anyone understood him – seemed at that time mere eccentricity or madness.

Yet Blake was not an originator of those ideas to which his genius gave such dynamic energy to change the course of history: rather he gathered the diverse strands of an excluded and rejected tradition into a new and powerful unity and coherence, loosing his Tyger upon the New Age which he declared was about to begin. Against the power and prestige of the scientific thought everywhere dominant Blake reaffirmed the traditional teaching that the ground and first principle of all creation is mind; or as he called it,

Imagination. He did not doubt that his message would sooner or later be understood, since he had clearly seen the fallacy, at that time undetected, in the prevailing positivist thought. He was following, besides, Swedenborg's prophecy of the advent of a 'new church' in 'the heavens' (the inner and spiritual worlds) in 1757, the year of Blake's birth. And indeed Swedenborg's astonishing visions of the inner worlds may be seen as a foreshadowing of the preoccupation of our own century with 'facts of mind'. Both prophets were in advance of history, for it is only in our own lifetime that the changes they foresaw have begun to come about.

Blake is even in a sense a poet of the twentieth century. During his lifetime his great prophecies existed only in those illuminated books of which he was himself author, engraver, printer, illustrator and publisher; selling only an occasional copy to friends who bought them as curiosities. In 1893 Edwin J. Ellis and W.B. Yeats published, in a limited edition (Quaritch), three volumes of text and commentaries; but it was only in 1925 that Keynes' edition made his works generally available. The renewal of the study of the inner worlds which has since taken place has made an understanding of Blake's thought at last possible. Jung's writings on the structure of the psyche have thrown light upon his mythological themes; but even more relevant to our present consideration of what Blake meant by the Imagination are the writings of Henry Corbin on the *mundus imaginalis*, the world of the 'Imaginal'; a theme to which we shall return.

Blake did not call in question the descriptive value of natural science; he could even write with poetic appreciation of the Newtonian heavens

Travelling in silent majesty along their order'd ways
In right lined paths outmeasur'd by proportions of number,
  weight
And measure, mathematic motion wondrous along the deep
(K287)

What he did question was the premiss, the Cartesian assumption that there are material bodies located in times and spaces external to consciousness; the false premiss which first separated mind from its object and made possible the materialist science which already in Blake's lifetime had undermined the foundations of spiritual knowledge. Henry Corbin, in his introduction to the second edition of *Corps Spirituelle et Terre Celeste** (his last statement on the nature of the *mundus imaginalis*) wrote:

> With the loss of the *Imagino vera* and the *mundus imaginalis* begins nihilism and agnosticism. This is why we say . . . that it is here necessary to forget everything the Aristotelian and related philosophers have had to say about the Imagination, considering it as a corporeal faculty.

This is precisely what Blake had struggled all his life – in discursive argument and memorable aphorism, in the action of his vast mythological drama, veiled in the deceptive simplicity of lyric verse, depicted in symbolic paintings and exemplified in the living of his life of poverty ennobled by vision – to communicate. In our own century the quantification of the universe has been extended to human consciousness itself. I recently found myself sitting, at a University banquet, beside a Professor of Physics who with evident pride told me that computers can now be made which can not only store information but which can also originate ideas in a way indistinguishable from human intuition. Blake, who wrote of natural science as the mortal sickness of the English nation ('the Giant Albion') whose 'machines are woven with his life', would not have been surprised at this modern idolatry. What was for Aristotle a convenient distinction made between mental and phenomenal worlds has proceeded to a denial, by positivist science, of any order other than its own. To Blake the corporeal body is 'the garment not

* Translated by Nancy Pearson as *Spiritual Body and Celestial Earth: From Mazdean Iran to Shī'ite Iran*, (Bollingen Series XCI : 2) Princeton University Press, 1977.

the man'; and in contrast with a science which supposes that knowledge is a function of sense-organs, he wrote: 'I would no more question my eye than I would question a window concerning a sight. I look through it, not with it.'

While the Deists of his day found no difficulty in reconciling their religion with the materialist premisses, Blake, in the lucidity of his imaginative grasp of the issues at stake, declared that this is impossible: not the discoveries of science but the premisses of materialism are heretical. He therefore called Bacon, Newton and Locke the 'three great teachers of Atheism or Satan's doctrine'. Atheism Blake defined as the worship of nature; 'for whoever believes in Nature said B. disbelieves in God – for Nature is the work of the Devil'. So Wordsworth's friend and diarist Crabb Robinson wrote in his Journal. In the myth of Urizen (the rational mentality) Blake embodies what he understands by the creation of 'nature' by the Devil; and in every allusion to the natural world so brought into apparent existence as an autonomous universe outside Imagination Blake describes it as a region of sorrow, cut off from the divine ground; it is Hell.

From his first writings to his last Blake was totally consistent. His thought is at all times based on the clear realization that 'All Things Exist in the Human Imagination'. (K707) The world we behold is a world of 'vision'; for

> . . . in your own Bosom you bear your Heaven
> And Earth & all you behold: tho' it appears Without, it is Within,
> In your Imagination. (K709)

When Blake was thirty-one he engraved his first illuminated book, three tractates against 'natural religion'. These are set forth as a discursive argument against Locke's thesis that man 'is only a natural organ subject to sense'. (K97) Whereas Locke based his system upon the premiss of a material order, Blake takes as his starting-point the mind which perceives. 'The true faculty of knowing is the faculty which experiences; This faculty I treat of.'

To Locke man is his natural body, a mirror or tablet upon which impressions are received from an external world. To Blake 'the true Man' is 'the Poetic Genius' or 'the Spirit of Prophecy' – Blake had not yet settled upon the term he was later to use consistently throughout the rest of his life, the Imagination. By this word Blake signified, as did Coleridge (his younger contemporary) an active and creative faculty, Coleridge's 'esemplastic power', 'My *shaping* spirit of Imagination'. For both poets Imagination is not passive but active, the divine creativity in man, the 'image' of God in which man is first created: for Coleridge, the individual portion of 'the adorable I AM'; for Blake the 'Divine Human', 'Jesus the Imagination'.

Blake's phrase, 'the true Man', is probably derived from his contemporary and acquaintance Thomas Taylor's Platonic translations and commentaries. According to Plato 'the true Man is intellect'. In preferring the terms 'Poetic Genius' and 'Spirit of Prophecy' and the Imagination, Blake is from the outset choosing a language more dynamic than that of the paradigmatic Platonic system. In this he may have been influenced by Jacob Boehme, whose writings he supremely admired. Blake's Imagination is less a principle than a Person, the human 'body' or 'body of Jesus', of which, as with Swedenborg's 'Grand Man of the Heavens', all human individuals are members; a Person living, active and creative. This body is not, of course, corporeal: the body of the Divine Humanity, as Swedenborg had insisted, is neither large nor small, nor of any dimension, being not subject to the Cartesian categories of space and body. This Swedenborgian and Blakean conception of the universe rather as a Person than as an object strikes the modern mind as strange; yet this has not been true of other periods and other civilizations. Henry Corbin, writing of the Iranian mysticism of the Zend-Avesta, describes a view of things very close to Blake's:

> To grasp the intentions which constituted that universe where the Earth is conceived, meditated, and encountered in

> the person of its Angel, we discover that it is much less a matter of answering questions concerning essences ('what is it?') than of questions concerning persons ('who is it?' 'to whom does it correspond?'). For example, *who* is the Earth, *who* are the Waters, the plants, the mountains, or *to whom* do they correspond? The answer to these questions makes present an imaginal Form, and that imaginal Form corresponds in each case to the presence of a certain state.

Blake also looks back to a Paradisal state in which humankind encountered earth and all creatures as living persons and not as lifeless objects; and laments the passing of that state brought about by the rending of the phenomena from the living Imagination in which they 'live and move and have their being'.

> A Rock, a Cloud, a Mountain,
> Were now not Vocal as in Climes of happy Eternity
> Where the lamb replies to the infant voice, & the lion to the man of years
> Giving them sweet instructions; where the Cloud, the River & the Field
> Talk with the husbandman & shepherd. (K315)

All things are living because their 'place' and their being participates in the life of the Imagination, the supreme Person. In answer to the poet's question, 'what is the material world and is it dead?', a spirit of vegetation replies, 'I'll shew you all alive/The world where every particle of dust breathes forth its joy.'

Before proceeding further we must give Blake's fullest and late definition of the Imagination:

> This world of Imagination is the world of Eternity; it is the divine bosom into which we shall all go after the death of the Vegetated body. This World of Imagination is Infinite & Eternal, whereas the world of Generation, or Vegetation, is Finite & Temporal. There Exist in that Eternal World the

> Permanent Realities of Every Thing which we see reflected in this Vegetable Glass of Nature. All things are comprehended in their Eternal Forms in the divine body of the Saviour, the True Vine of Eternity, The Human Imagination, who appear'd to Me as Coming to Judgment among his Saints & throwing off the Temporal that the Eternal might be Establish'd. (K605–6)

Whereas for Locke mind is the passive mirror of a mechanized nature, for Blake Imagination is both Person and 'place' where all beings and events are situated. Striking mutual confirmation is again to be found in the comparison between Blake's Imagination and Henry Corbin's *mundus imaginalis* as described in the light of his studies in Iranian mysticism, a tradition totally unknown to Blake, although the Platonic tradition underlies both. This *mundus imaginalis* is the 'place' of all spiritual events. Corbin writes: 'Therefore if one deprives all this of its proper domain, which is the active imagination, nothing of all this any longer has a "place" and in consequence cannot "take place". It is now only the "imaginary" of fiction.' 'Imaginary' in the sense of fictitious, non-existent, is exactly what Urizen considered the Imagination to be; a view of positivist science concisely summed up in the phrase '*The Spectre is the Man; The rest is only delusion & fancy.*' (K273)—the 'Spectre' being the corporeal man. Against this view Blake fought his lifelong battle.

Another source of his concept of the Imagination was doubtless the *Hermetica*. In the Tenth Book (117–19) he would have read:

> All things are in God, not as lying in a Place; for a Place is both a Body, and unmoveable, and those things that are there placed have no motion. For they lie otherwise in that which is unbodily, than in the fantasy or to appearance. Consider him that contains all things, and understand that nothing is more capacious, than that which is incorporeal, nothing more swift, nothing more powerful.

Blake was also familiar with the writings of the eighteenth century Irish philosopher Berkeley, who himself drew many arguments for his own unitive philosophy from the *Hermetica*. Blake knew also (again in Thomas Taylor's translations) Plotinus' arguments against the substantial existence of 'matter', which he calls a *non-ens*, possessing only an apparent existence. He was, besides, a follower of Swedenborg, for whom the inner 'worlds' had opened in a revelatory manner. Blake's declaration of his own prophetic task has an echo of Swedenborg's existential revelation:

I rest not from my great task!
To open the Eternal Worlds, to open the immortal Eyes
Of Man inwards into the Worlds of Thought, into Eternity
Ever expanding in the Bosom of God, the Human Imagination.
(K623)

Blake in an early poem, the *Book of Urizen*, describes in the form of a myth the creation of the corporeal world. Before Urizen began his labours there was no temporal world:

Earth was not: nor globes of attraction;
The will of the Immortal expanded
Or contracted his all flexible senses;
Death was not, but eternal life sprung. (K223)

Blake, we must remember, is writing of creation not in terms of matter but of consciousness – 'the faculty which experiences'. In a passage written many years later, on his painting of a Vision of the Last Judgement, he expands this theme:

Many suppose that before the Creation All was Solitude & Chaos. This is the most pernicious Idea that can enter the Mind, as it takes away all sublimity from the Bible & Limits All Existence to Creation & to Chaos, To the Time & Space fixed by the Corporeal Vegetative Eye, & leaves the Man who entertains such an Idea the habitation of Unbelieving

> demons. Eternity Exists, and All things in Eternity, Independent of Creation. (K614)

Blake's 'unbelieving demons' are the same disbelief which, as Corbin points out, persuades us that the Imagination – the *mundus imaginalis* – is purely imaginary and non-existent. Blake's logic is sound; it is the argument of all who are aware of the reality of this incorporeal 'place' where spiritual history (of the kind described for example in the Bible) 'takes place'. The mind of the ratio, of the empirical ego, creates outside the Imagination the externality of the corporeal world in what Blake calls 'the void outside existence', 'the petrific abominable chaos', 'a void immense, wild, dark and deep / Where nothing was', 'a wide world of solid obstruction', 'a horrid bottomless vacuity'. It is above all a world of death. Imagination is in its nature a world of immortal life; being incorporeal, not located in space or in time, and not therefore subject to change, generation and decay. Blake affirms without doubt that it is the world 'into which we shall all go after the death of the Vegetated body'. Corbin affirms the same of the Imaginal world:

> We take the decisive step in the metaphysics of the imaginal and of the Imagination from the time we admit . . . that the imaginative power is a purely spiritual faculty, independent of the physical organism and in consequence surviving it.

Blake also called the Imagination 'the land of life'; and in his understanding it is by identifying 'the true Man' with his mortal body that an understanding and knowledge of immortality has been lost. Deism replaced knowledge of the world of Imagination with a teaching that the mortal body has an 'afterlife'; it is in Urizen's world that men are taught

> That an Eternal life awaits the worms of sixty winters
> In an allegorical abode where existence hath never come.
> (K240)

This is natural religion's travesty of the true teaching of immortality. Blake for his part dismissed it as nonsense.

Blake has depicted as well as described the 'eternals' gazing down in horror into the Abyss, or shown them suspended head downwards in the void as they undergo a 'shrinking' and metamorphosis from the 'human' (that is, imaginative) into the 'serpent' form of the 'mortal worm' – natural man.

We must remember at all times that a 'world' for Blake is situated not in Cartesian space but in consciousness; therefore every change of consciousness changes the world. The positivist scientific ideology shrinks man from the unbounded being of Imagination into mortality; of which the serpent is Blake's symbol. In *Genesis* the Serpent is condemned to crawl on its belly on the earth, and to eat dust; as Blake writes

> For dust & Clay is the Serpent's meat,
> Which never was made for Man to Eat. (K755)

The food of the 'true man' is 'The Bread of sweet Thought & the Wine of Delight'. (K800) In Urizen's world men become mortal worms, and dust-eaters. This comes about through the shrinking of perceptions; the 'eyes' of the 'inhabitants' of Urizen's cities are 'shrunken', their 'heavens' become 'streaky slime':

> . . . for their eyes
> Grew small like the eyes of a man,
> And in reptile forms shrinking together,
> Of seven feet stature they remain'd. (K236)

They 'shrunk up from existence' and 'forgot their eternal life',

> . . . shut in narrow doleful form
> Creeping in reptile flesh upon the bosom of the ground.
> (K484)

Blake asks:

> Can such an Eye judge of the stars? & looking thro' its tubes
> Measure the sunny rays that point their spears on Udanadan?
> Can such an Ear, fill'd with the vapours of the yawning pit,
> Judge of the pure melodious harp struck by a hand divine?
>
> (K485)

The universe, according to Orphic tradition, is Apollo's lyre whose harmonies are a divine utterance, a divine communication of meaning and beauty. By banishing the phenomena from the Imagination – the 'faculty which experiences' – they are emptied of all significance, retaining only a quantitative existence. 'What is within is now seen without' and humankind 'raw to the hungry wind' live no longer in immeasurable incorporeal spaces but in 'a little and dark Land'. Yet even from this fallen race the world of Imagination is not wholly withdrawn; within every creature 'eternity expands'. The mortal worm, oppressed by Urizen, natural reason, has at all times access to the indwelling Imagination:

> He wither'd up the Human Form
> By laws of sacrifice for sin,
> Till it became a Mortal Worm,
> But O! translucent all within. (K651)

It remains for Urizen, in his new world of materialized nature, to invent a system of 'laws of nature', autonomous and self-contained; forgetting that, as the Platonic and all other spiritual traditions have held,

> . . . every Natural Effect has a Spiritual Cause, and Not
> A Natural; for a Natural Cause only seems: it is a Delusion
> Of Ulro & a ratio of the perishing Vegetable Memory.
>
> (K513)

'Losing the Divine Vision that all behold and live thereby' Urizen exchanges eternity for 'futurity', infinity for unending space.

Holding as he did that knowledge is a mode of consciousness, Blake does not present us with Urizen's arguments, but depicts rationalist materialism as a state of mind, of being. He depicts Urizen as a travesty of God the Father, anxious, purblind, laborious, a joyless tyrant. In the void of 'futurity' and of ever-elusive matter, Reason, with infinite labour, constructs a 'world of rocky destiny', 'Petrifying the Human Imagination into rock and sand.' He invents the 'laws of nature', based upon weight and measure, extension and duration within the Cartesian categories,

> . . . Mathematic Holiness, Length Bredth & Highth,
> Calling the Human Imagination, which is the Divine Vision
> & Fruition
> In which Man liveth eternally, madness and blasphemy against
> Its own Qualities. (K521)

In this world 'outside existence' creatures become mere things, emptied of life and meaning. The animals 'wander away from man' in 'sullen droves', and nature becomes emptied of all but quantitative significance. Inevitably human beings also become externalized and quantified:

> His Children exil'd from his breast pass to and fro before him,
> His birds are silent in his hills, flocks die beneath his branches.
> (K641)

Separated from life, nature is no longer experienced but only observed:

> . . . the Forests fled,
> The Corn-fields & the breathing Gardens outside separated,
> The Sea, the Stars, the Sun, the Moon. (K643)

The creatures, man's companions in Paradise, 'wander away into a distant night'.

The rationalist mentality of Urizen is sustained by a passion for the accumulation of the only kind of 'knowledge' it recognises. In order, as Blake says, to 'avert his own despair' Urizen sets out on the immense labours of investigation of his 'dens'—the great adventure of scientific discovery. Blake represents him carrying with him his heavy 'books' in which he keeps his records. Yet to the natural universe reason can find neither end nor resting-place in a '... world of Cumbrous wheels, / Circle o'er Circle, ... / '... down falling thro' immensity ever and ever.' / (K316–7) There is no point at which the 'more' or quantitative knowledge becomes the 'all' of wisdom. Blake describes Urizen's explorations as taking him through the outer spaces of Newtonian astronomy, but our own century has found within the sub-atomic world the same boundless void and 'dark vacuity'. The scientific mind sets out to 'conquer' nature; yet Urizen is not able to 'calm the Elements, because himself was subject'. This is necessarily so within the positivist definition of man as 'a natural organ subject to sense'. Incorporeal Imagination is not subject to the elements, or at their mercy as, finally, the materialist must always remain. Whatever 'progress' may be made towards some scientific Utopia it can never in the nature of things be reached, 'nature' being a world of mutability and mortality in terms of its own definitions. Therefore Urizen is condemned to unending 'research' and 'progress', 'urg'd by necessity to keep / The evil day afar', knowing that at the heart of his philosophy lies the *nihil* which the 'reasoning spectre' never ceases to whisper to the English nation:

> I am your Rational Power, O Albion, & that Human Form
> You call Divine is but a Worm seventy inches long
> That creeps forth in a night & is dried in the morning sun
>
> (K659)

The great cities and triumphs of technological construction are but worm-casts that time will obliterate. 'Futurity' enables Urizen to postpone, but not to avert the knowledge that 'despair is his eternal lot'.

But upon his rational laws Urizen prides himself; and above all on account of the universality and uniformity of their operation. They permit no exceptions or variety. Throughout his world he has imposed

> One command, one joy, one desire,
> One curse, one weight, one measure,
> One King, one God, one Law. (K224)

—for rational knowledge is uniform, predictable, objective; a philosophy condemned in Blake's aphorism, 'One Law for the Lion & Ox is Oppression' (K158), illustrated by the terrifying depiction of Nebuchadnezzar condemned to eat grass.

I hope that it is by now clear that Blake was not making a vital issue out of what is in reality a mere matter of terms and definitions. Some might ask what difference it can possibly make, since the perception and experience of the world is in either case the same, whether we regard the phenomena as material or mental. To Blake the 'wrenching apart' of the *unus mundus* is, as in his myth he describes it, an unhealed wound in consciousness itself. The healing of that separation was for him essential 'for the sake of eternal life', as he writes. It is not in facts but in experience that knowledge consists: knowledge is not separable from life; and Urizen's universe is constructed 'outside eternity'—outside the life of the Imagination. Our world depends not, as Locke had taught, upon the reception of stimuli from a mechanized universe but upon the 'faculty which experiences', the mind of the beholder: 'a fool sees not the same tree as a wise man sees':

> ... to the Eyes of the Man of Imagination, Nature is Imagination itself. As a man is, So he Sees. As the Eye is formed, such are its Powers ... To Me This World is all One continued Vision of Fancy or Imagination. (K793)

In defining the world as 'one continued vision' Blake follows Berkeley, who had also tried to heal the division between perception and its object. Blake might well have been paraphrasing Berkeley when he wrote:

> Mental Things are alone Real; what is call'd Corporeal, Nobody Knows of its Dwelling-Place: it is in Fallacy & its Existence an Imposture. Where is the Existence Out of mind and Thought? Where is it but in the mind of a Fool? (K617)

For Berkeley all things exist in the mind of God; Blake went further, declaring that the human Imagination is the divine in man. An eighteenth century bishop may have hesitated openly to take the further step made by Blake. Blake certainly had the authority of the *Hermetica*; in the section entitled 'Poimandres' both Blake and Berkeley would have read 'That which in thee seeth and heareth, the word of the Lord, and the Mind, the Father, God, Differeth not the One from the Other.' In his uncompromising affirmation of the identity of the human Imagination with the divine Person and the divine world Blake is at once affirming sacred tradition, and proclaiming the doctrine of the New Age which he foresaw must supercede what Yeats has called the 'three provincial centuries' of naïve materialism.

To the 'man of Imagination' nature lives with the life of the Imagination which perceives it; and thus the experiences of the materialist and of the man of Imagination are incommensurable, different not in degree but in kind. Defending the art which springs from the Imagination as against the 'distinct and inferior' art produced by copying nature, Blake insists that 'allegory' (derived from nature) and 'Visions of Imagination ought to be known as Two Distinct Things, & so call'd for the Sake of Eternal Life'. (K604–5) For the sake of eternal life because Imagination *is* eternal life. Thus when Blake speaks of the dust as 'all alive' he is not personifying a particle of dust that is really lifeless: that is what he means by allegory. Copiers of 'nature' would doubtless see it so, for Urizen has his artists as well as his scientists. But Blake affirms that these particles are not only alive, but, because they have their existence within the human Imagination, are also human:

> Each grain of Sand,
> Every Stone on the Land,
> Each rock & each hill,
> Each fountain & rill,
> Each herb & each tree,
> Mountain, hill, earth & sea,
> Cloud, Meteor & Star
> Are Men Seen Afar. (K804–5)

> For all are Men in Eternity, Rivers, Mountains, Cities, Villages,
> All are Human, & when you enter into their Bosoms you walk
> In Heavens & Earths, as in your own Bosom you bear your Heaven
> And Earth and all you behold; tho' it appears Without, it is Within,
> In your Imagination, of which this World of Mortality is but a Shadow. (K709)

Blake has been called a 'mystic'—untruly I believe if the word is understood in any world-negating sense; and a 'visionary', with implications of paranormal perception, real or unreal. But Blake's world of vision is not 'another' world; it is this world, seen differently. Blake's inner world *is* the outer world. His 'visions of eternity' are what everyman sees around him every day, as he stands at the centre of his own universe in which 'every space is visionary':

> And every Space that a Man views around his dwelling-place
> Standing on his own roof or on his garden on a mount
> Of twenty-five cubits in height, such space is his Universe:
> And on its verge the Sun rises & sets, the Clouds bow
> To meet the flat Earth & the Sea in such an order'd Space:

On all sides, & the two Poles turn on their valves of gold;
And if he move his dwelling-place, his heavens also move
Where'er he goes, & all his neighbourhood bewail his loss.
Such are the Spaces called Earth & such its dimension.

(K516)

All spaces and times exist within the mind, and are 'flexible' and ever-various. Urizen prided himself upon the unity and immutability of his 'One Law for the Lion & Ox'; the universe of science is a single universe. The Imagination is a plurality of universes; or, rather, 'nature' imposes one object upon many minds; whereas in the world of Imagination the one Mind creates innumerable universes. Within the living unity of Imagination moves an endless succession of 'visions' or 'worlds' of thought: 'Ever expanding in the Bosom of God, the Human Imagination'. (K623) The times and spaces of Imagination, being incorporeal, are not natural distances or durations; no more so than are the spaces and durations of our dreams.

In the eternal world Los and Enitharmon (the agents of time and space in Blake's myth)

... walk'd forth on the dewy Earth
Contracting or expanding their all flexible senses
At will to murmur in the flowers small as the honey bee,
At will to stretch across the heavens & step from star to star.

(K288)

Coleridge wrote that he had failed to make Wordsworth understand that he could leap along the line of a distant mountain; for Wordsworth (poet as he was of Newtonian 'nature') could not understand how it is possible to 'be' in a place otherwise than bodily. Doubtless Coleridge knew, as Blake also did, a passage from the *Hermetica* (Book 10, 120-22) in which Blake's doctrine of Imagination as the place of all spaces is beautifully set forth:

> And judge of this by thyself, command thy Soul to go to India, and sooner than thou canst bid it, it will be there. Bid it likewise pass over the ocean, and suddenly it will be there; not as passing from place to place, but suddenly it will be there. Command it to fly into Heaven, and it will need no Wings, neither shall anything hinder it.

How easy it is in childhood to make a forest of the grass, or to descend into the fiery caverns of the smouldering coal! It is this gift of 'reverie' that initiated Gaston Bachelard into the interior spaces of gems, acorns, the roots of trees, the interior of things; the rapturous ascensions of the soul into the heights of air with the skylark, or descents into underworlds of ocean or within the earth where body cannot accompany thought.

Every creature is indeed a boundless universe; and in *The Marriage of Heaven and Hell* Blake asks:

> How do you know but ev'ry Bird that cuts the airy way,
> Is an immense world of delight, clos'd by your senses
> five? (K150)

In *Visions of the Daughters of Albion* Blake contrasts Locke's spaces of a science-fiction world,

> . . . spread in the infinite microscope
> In places yet unvisited by the voyager, and in worlds
> Over another kind of seas (K192)

with the unbounded nature of life itself, the endless variety of life. Sense-organs are much the same in chicken and hawk and pigeon, mouse and frog, ass and camel, wolf and tiger; how then explain in physical terms why

> . . . their habitations
> And their pursuits as different as their forms and as their
> joys. (K191)

They live in different worlds indeed; but without needing to cross outer (or inner) 'space' to find them. Every creature lives in the total freedom of its Imagination; and Blake concludes his marvellous poetic evocation of the boundless variety of worlds in words that are his answer to Urizen's One Law for the Lion and Ox:

> And trees & birds & beasts & men behold their eternal joy.
> Arise, you little glancing wings, and sing your infant joy!
> Arise, and drink your bliss, for every thing that lives is holy.
>
> (K195)

Blake makes one final claim on behalf of the Imagination in his repeated affirmation that 'every thing that lives is holy'. By this he meant that life itself, as such, is sacred. But what is the meaning of these words? Is it not a matter of opinion, whether or not life is 'holy', and is not this a mere value judgment which we are free to accept or to reject?

In terms of material science to say that life is 'holy' has no meaning at all. Indeed what science calls 'life' is not so in Blake's sense of the word, but only one among other possible ways in which matter can behave, a process which can be described and quantified. If you say 'life' to a physiologist he will speak of chemistry, or of electrical waves given off by the brain; a geneticist will talk about DNA or something of that sort. But in Blake's terms these are not 'life' at all; nor is there any continuity between 'life' as something experienced and such accompanying physical phenomena. These are incommensurable. Electrical discharges may indicate that a subject is dreaming but it can tell us nothing of the dream itself, its fields and gardens, its imagined persons and events. The difference is not in degree but in kind: 'nature' may be measured but not experienced; experience is immeasurable.

Urizen uses the word 'holy' in quite another sense. He regards measurement as sacred in the sense of being beyond and above argument or doubt, not under any circumstances to be called in question: 'Satan's mathematic holiness, Length Bredth & Highth'.

Or laws may decree that Caesar's statue is to be worshipped on pain of death, or a building consecrated to some cult. In these cases 'holiness' is imputed to some person, place or thing, but is not inherent in it. But holiness, in the sense in which Blake declares life to be holy, is inherent in the living Imagination, which is, both by definition and by experience, the 'divine body', the 'holy land', the *temenos*, the sanctuary. The sense of the holy is the experience itself. Indeed the holy exists only in being experienced. The ultimate condemnation of the positivist philosophy of the modern West is that it has imposed upon great masses of mankind an ideology which precludes the experiencing of the most profound regions of the soul. Perhaps even a majority of the atheist West suffer throughout adult life a deprivation of the soul, never knowing the experience of the numinous, of awe, of that overwhelming joy and fear and wonder which it is natural for us to feel in the presence of the holy; never know the experience of worship, are never overwhelmed, as Moses was, in the presence of a bush in the desert burning with the fire of God; or the terror of Arjuna when the Lord Krishna revealed his myriad-formed presence. Since these *are* experiences which fall within the range of our humanity—have been known to countless men and women throughout the world's history—it is a mutilation, a deadly sickness, a spiritual death (and such Blake called it) which deprives so many of the highest human fulfilment. That is what Blake meant by writing that his words are for our 'eternal salvation'; for he never exaggerated in these matters: he meant exactly what he said. Eternity is the Imaginative vision; and Imagination is 'the Saviour'. His lifelong intellectual labours were to bring back, to make accessible, the experience of the holiness of life; all but lost to the English nation under the domination of materialist atheism. And yet the sense of the holiness of life is the human norm, 'the human existence itself'. The Western materialist ideology is a mutilation of consciousness, precluding the experience of a living world, making of knowledge a formula and not an experience. Blake uses the example of music: science can describe 'discord and harmony' for these are quantifiable; but of melody can tell us nothing; for melody can only be experienced in terms of meaning, by the Imagination which responds to the universe as 'a harp struck by a hand divine'.

It is hard to see how greater 'truth' can be claimed by a philosophy which narrows the range of possible human experience, which prevents certain potentialities of the soul from ever being realized. Blake calls Urizen 'the idiot questioner' who can question but cannot answer; the man of Imagination, by contrast, will never

> Charge Visionaries with deceiving
> Or call Men wise for not Believing. (K756)

Blake and Maya

In his own lifetime few understood or heeded Blake's radical calling in question of those natural sciences which in terms of material prosperity seemed so beneficial. Nor indeed was it the observations of the scientists that Blake questioned but the whole post-Cartesian concept of nature as a self-operating mechanism, existing in natural space outside and apart from mind. His own view of nature is the orthodoxy (so to say) of the Perennial Philosophy as it had reached him through those many underground streams which have continued to nourish the imagination of European artists and poets; a view so close to the Indian view of nature as *maya* as to raise the question of Blake's own debt to that tradition.

When Blake declared that all religions are one, he doubtless included the religions of India. Charles Wilkins, at the request of Warren Hastings, had made the first English translation of the *Bhagavad-Gita*, published in 1785. This work had impressed Blake sufficiently to inspire a work (now lost) entitled *The Bramins—A Drawing*, listed in the catalogue of his one exhibition (in 1809), of which he wrote: 'The subject is, Mr. Wilkin translating the Geeta'. Blake would have found no difficulty in recognizing in the figure of Krishna the 'true Man' and the Divine Humanity whom he himself identified with Jesus; Krishna says of himself:

> I am the creation and the dissolution of the whole universe.

> There is not any greater than I; and all things hang on me, even as precious gems upon a string. I am moisture in the water, light in the sun and moon, invocation in the *Vēds*, sound in the firmament, human nature in mankind, sweet-smelling savour in the earth, glory in the source of light; in all things I am life . . . (Lecture VIII)

And again:

> Behold, in this my body the whole world animate and inanimate, and all things else thou hast a mind to see.

And Arjuna

> beheld within the body of the God of Gods, standing together, the whole universe divided forth into its vast variety. He was overwhelmed with wonder, and every hair was raised on end.

The majestic vision continues in the words of Arjuna:

> I see thyself, on all sides, of infinite shape, formed with abundant arms and bellies, and mouths, and eyes; but I can neither discover thy beginning, thy middle, or again thy end. O universal Lord, form of the universe! I see thee with a crown, and armed with club and *Chakra*, a mass of glory, darting refulgent beams around. I see thee, difficult to be seen, shining on all sides with light immeasurable.
>
> (Lecture XI)

Was the vision of Arjuna one element which contributed to Blake's understanding of the Imagination as at once the person and the place of the universe?

Near the end of his life, writing in the margins of Berkeley's *Siris*, a work he must have loved for its radical challenge of the materialist philosophy, Blake wrote: 'Imagination is the Divine Body in Every Man . . . The All in Man. The Divine Image or Imagination'. What

Berkeley affirms of God, Blake affirms of the Imagination, the God within. Beside Berkeley's words 'God knoweth all things as pure mind or intellect, but nothing by sense, nor in nor through a sensory' Blake wrote 'Imagination or the Human Eternal Body in Every Man'. (K776)

Both Berkeley and Blake knew the *Hermetica*, that blend of neo-Platonic and Egyptian gnostic thought, translated in the seventeenth century by Dr. Everard as *The Divine Pymander of Hermes Trismegistus*. In the eleventh tractate the Poimander, the 'shepherd of men' speaks – as Krishna to Arjuna – to Hermes:

> Methought I saw one of an exceeding great stature, and of an infinite greatness, call me by my name . . . Then said I, *Who art Thou*? I am, quoth he, *Poemander*, the mind of the great *Lord*, the most mighty and absolute *Emperor*: I know what thou wouldst have, and I am always present with thee.

The Poimander presently declares himself:

> I am that Light, the Mind, thy God . . .
> How is that? quoth I?
> Thus, replied he, understand it: *That which in thee seeth and heareth, the Word of the Lord, and the Mind of the Father, God, differ not one from another; and the union of these is Life* . . . These things I understood, seeing the Word, or Pymander; and when I was mightily amazed, he said again unto me, Hast thou seen in thy mind that Archetypal Form which was before the interminated and infinite beginning?

Berkeley based his argument against the post-Cartesian notion of natural space on the *Hermetica*:

> It is observed in the *Asclepian Dialogue* that the word *space* or *place* hath by itself no meaning, and again that it is impossible to understand what space alone or pure space is. And Plotinus acknowledgeth no place but soul or mind, expressly affirming

> that the soul is not in the world, but the world in the soul. And farther, the place of soul, saith he, is not body, but soul is in mind, and body is in soul. [*Siris* para. 270]

The passage to which Berkeley refers is in the dialogue between Asclepias and Hermes:

> Asclepias: What shall we call the place in which the Universe is moved?
> Hermes: Call it incorporeal, O Asclepias.
> Asclepias: What is that incorporeal or unbodily?
> Hermes: The Mind or Reason, the whole, wholly comprehending in itself, free from all Body, undeceivable, invisible, impassible from a Body itself, standing fast in itself, capable of all things

Again, in Book 10: 'All things are in God, not as lying in a place . . . Consider him that contains all things, and understand that nothing is more capacious than that which is incorporeal.'

In the premiss which holds matter to comprise a universe in its own right, apart from mind or spirit, Blake saw the fatal deviation of Western culture; and about the nature of the perceptible world his great mythological drama of the Giant Albion revolves.

It must seem from an Indian standpoint almost incredible that Blake had to labour as he did against attitudes so rigidly set in a quantitative mode, to make clear something so simple and self-evident. Of the greatness of the loss, the narrowing and diminishment of life resulting from the rise of materialism Blake was bitterly aware:

> What seems to Be, Is, To those to whom
> It seems to Be, & is productive of the most dreadful
> Consequences to those to whom it seems to Be, even of
> Torments, Despair, Eternal Death.

But, the passage continues,

. . . the Divine Mercy
Steps beyond and Redeems Man in the Body of Jesus. Amen.
And Length, Bredth, Highth again Obey the Divine Vision.
(K663–4)

His meaning is precise: the 'Body of Jesus' is the Imagination, which can redeem humanity from the quantitative perception of the world. 'The mind altering alters all', Blake wrote:

He who Doubts from what he sees
Will ne'er Believe, do what you Please.
If the Sun & Moon should doubt,
They'd immediately Go out. (K432)

This is Berkeley's argument—sensible things do really exist because they are perceived: 'Their *esse* is *percipi*'. And Yeats was but echoing Berkeley and Blake when he wrote:

God-appointed Berkeley that proved all things a dream,
That this pragmatical, preposterous pig of a world, its farrow
that so solid seem,
Must vanish on the instant if the mind but change its theme.
('Blood and the Moon')

The author of the *Bhagavad-Gita* too was aware that more was at stake than a change of opinion: did not Arjuna's hair stand on end in the overwhelming realization of that change of consciousness Blake calls the 'Last Judgment'? For to Blake the ultimate enlightenment is nothing less than this transforming vision. His final words on the 'Last Judgment' are concerned only with this transformation of consciousness itself:

Error is Created. Truth is Eternal. Error, or Creation, will be Burned up, & then, & not till Then, Truth or Eternity will appear. It is Burnt up the Moment Men cease to behold it. (K617)

It was Berkeley who broke down the Cartesian distinction between primary and secondary qualities, and argued that not only did colour, scent and the like exist only within the mind, but also space itself, and therefore also matter itself. For

> though we should grant this outward substance [Matter, that is] may possibly exist, *Yet where can it be supposed to be?* That it exists not in the mind is agreed and that it exists not in place is no less certain: since all (place or) extension exists only in the mind . . . It remains therefore that it exists nowhere at all.

Blake was repeating Berkeley's argument when he wrote:

> Mental Things are alone Real; what is call'd Corporeal, Nobody Knows of its Dwelling Place: it is in Fallacy, & its Existence an Imposture. Where is the Existence Out of Mind or Thought? Where is it but in the Mind of a Fool? (K617)

Berkeley particularizes:

> It is indeed an opinion strangely prevailing amongst men, that houses, mountains, rivers, and in a word all sensible objects have an existence natural or real distinct from their being perceived by the understanding. (*Principles of Human Knowledge* para. 4)

And again Blake adds impassioned feeling to Berkeley's thought:

> For all are Men in Eternity, Rivers, Mountains, Cities,
> Villages,
> All are Human, & when you enter into their Bosoms you walk
> In Heavens & Earths, as in your own Bosom you bear your
> Heaven
> And Earth & all you behold; tho' it appears Without, it is
> Within,
> In your Imagination, of which this World of Mortality is but
> a Shadow. (K709)

We have still to consider the element of direct Indian influence on Blake's thought, and especially upon his figure of Vala, 'the Goddess Nature', whose name is taken from her veil, symbol of the illusory and ever-varying appearances of the natural world. Yet striking as these resemblances may be, there are, again, threads of continuity linking Blake's Vala with those veiled goddesses of the Mediterranean whose links with India are in turn lost in antiquity.

There are, in Blake's mythological system, two feminine figures, each of whom has given her name to one of his three major Prophetic Books: Jerusalem, mother of souls, and Vala, mother of bodies or 'garments'; 'For Vala produc'd the Bodies, Jerusalem gave the Souls' (K640). Vala's only reality is as the 'shadow' of Jerusalem, a reflection of soul cast in the 'Vegetable Glass' of nature. She is therefore called the 'shadowy female', who becomes animated with a perverse life of her own. Thus the two goddesses are in a sense one. Plotinus, in *Ennead* 3, Book 8, *On Nature, Contemplation and the One*, of which Blake's one-time friend Thomas Taylor the Platonist made a paraphrase translation, writes of the desire of the soul of Nature to contemplate herself. This causes her to 'relinquish part of herself' into externality in order to behold as a 'spectacle' her seminal reasons in the mirror of nature, 'as if different from herself'. In the same way Vala is related to Jerusalem as shadow to substance. She herself has no substantiality, as Blake continually stresses, in such passages as:

> Vala is but thy Shadow, O thou loveliest among women!
> A shadow animated by thy tears, O mournful Jerusalem!
> Why wilt thou give to her a Body whose life is but a Shade?
> Her joy and love, a shade, a shade of sweet repose:
> But animated and vegetated she is a devouring worm.
>
> (K631)

Blake invariably describes the physical body as 'the garment, not the Man'; and in this sense, Vala *is* her veil. In *The Gates of Paradise*

Blake writes of the incarnation of the Divine Humanity in a physical body taking place

> Lest the Sexual Garments sweet
> Should grow a devouring Winding sheet. (K771)

According to mankind's spiritual condition (individually as well as culturally) the harmony between body and soul, substance and shadow, fluctuates. Thus Blake recalls his own early married happiness in Lambeth, the place of his own early home near Albion's river, the Thames:

> He [Albion] found Jerusalem upon the River of his City, soft
> repos'd
> In the arms of Vala, assimilating in one with Vala,
> The Lilly of Havilah, and they sang soft thro' Lambeth's vales
> In a sweet moony night & silence that they had created
> With a blue sky spread over with wings and a mild moon.
> (K642)

Jerusalem tells Vala that she is most beautiful and desirable when the soul is sheltered in her veil:

> When Albion rent thy beautiful net of gold and silver twine,
> Thou hadst woven it with art, thou hadst caught me in the bands
> Of love, thou refusedst to let me go: Albion beheld thy beauty,
> Beautiful thro' our Love's comeliness, beautiful thro' pity.
> The Veil shone with thy brightness in the eyes of Albion
> Because it inclos'd pity & love, because we lov'd one-another.
> (K643)

Separated from the soul, animated with an unnatural life of her own, Vala is cruel, destructive, a goddess of death. She, as sexuality, is the cause of the fall of Albion who is seduced by the shadowy veil of bodily nature, and thus becomes through sexual enslavement subject to the cruel tyranny of the body. Vala is also the agent of war and bloodshed, because she is the weaver of mortal bodies who, without spiritual life, become warring armies. Jerusalem asks her:

> Tell me, O Vala, thy purposes; tell me wherefore thy shuttles
> Drop with the gore of the slain, why Euphrates is red with blood,
> Wherefore in dreadful majesty & beauty outside appears
> Thy Masculine from thy Feminine, hardening against the
> heavens
> To devour the Human! . . .
> O Vala! Humanity is far above
> Sexual organization. (K721)

But to Vala the natural body is all and sexuality becomes a murderous machine generating bodies for war and death. She knows only the natural law, unaware that man is a spiritual being:

> Her Hand is a Court of Justice: her Feet two Armies in Battle:
> Storms & Pestilence in her Locks, & in her Loins Earthquake
> And Fire & the Ruin of Cities & Nations & families (K698)

Indian mythology is realistic in its conception of this dark and murderous side of the feminine principle in the person of Kali, a realism with no parallel in the Christian world of Blake's time and place. To Vala 'the Human is but a Worm' and 'the Human Divine is Woman's Shadow, a Vapour in the summer's heat'. Thus Vala, the shadow, herself claims to be the substance. Western man, falling in love with nature, the shadow, becomes at last her slave.

The veil of Vala is nature; and as such the attribute of many veiled goddesses of the Mediterranean—Juno, Minerva, Demeter, Isis; Psyche, the soul, at her marriage is veiled, as are Christian brides to this day. The Shulamite in the Song of Solomon has also her veil and complains that 'the keepers of the walls took away my veil from me'. Behind this image lies perhaps a recollection of the goddess Ishtar whose seven veils were taken from her on her journey into the Underworld. Persephone was occupied in weaving a veil for Demeter, the great mother-goddess, when she fell into the power of Hades; and this web was, according to Thomas

Taylor the Platonist 'the web in which Proserpine had displayed all the fair variety of the material world, through which the soul becomes ensnared with the beauty of imaginative forms' (*Dissertation on the Mysteries of Eleusis* p.98). Blake himself wrote that 'Eternity is in love with the productions of Time' – Plato's 'image of eternity', which he calls 'the most beautiful of *generated* things'.

Since the veil is nature, it may also be called a 'garden'; and Blake writes of Vala's 'garden', a 'garden of delight'. The image is taken above all from Boehme, who wrote of the creation by seven 'fountain spirits' of which the 'garden' (-spirit) is the seventh – the Malkuth of the Cabbalistic Tree of God:

> For it is the proper House and Habitation of the six Spirits, which they continually build according to their Pleasure, or as a Garden of Delight, into which the Master of it *sows* all manner of Seeds, according to his Pleasure, and enjoys the Fruit of it. (*Aurora* 16. 21–22)

These 'Seeds' are of course the 'seminal reasons' of Plato and Plotinus, which inform the world of matter, itself devoid of form but the recipient of the souls of every species. Blake uses Boehme's phrase when he writes: 'O Vala, once I liv'd in a garden of delight' (K339) (The speaker is Albion). Another beautiful variant of this seventh spirit of the garden is the Thalia of Thomas Vaughan, the alchemist; she has a veil that not only 'looks like', but is, 'lilies in a field of grass' (*Lumen de Lumine* p.3).

Of these figures of mother Nature the most august is Isis herself, who bears the two symbols of the mirror and the veil; beautifully described by Apuleius, himself an initiate of the mysteries of Isis, this veil was

> of fine silke yeelding divers colours, sometime yellow, sometime rosie, sometime flamy, and sometime (which troubled my spirit sore) darke and obscure, covered with a blacke robe in manner of a shield, and pleated in most subtill fashion at

> the skirts of her garments, the welts appeared comely, whereas here and there the starres glimpsed, and in the middle of them was placed the Moone, which shone like a flame of fire, round about the robe was a coronet or garland made with flowres and fruits. (*Metamorphoses* Book 11, Chapter 47, trs. Adlington)

Isis declares her nature:

> I am she that is the natural mother of all things, mistresse and governesse of all the elements, the initial progeny of worlds, chiefe of powers divine.

Plutarch explains the multi-coloured garment of the goddess:

> The robes of *Isis* are dyed with a great variety of colours, her power being wholly conversant about *Matter*, which becomes all things and admits all things, light and darkness, day and night, fire and water, life and death, beginning and end. (*Treatise of Isis & Osiris*)

And Plutarch records the inscription upon the base of the statue of Minerva at Sais: 'I am every thing that has been, that is, and that shall be: nor has any mortal ever yet been able to discover what is under my veil'.

This remains no less true of modern science than for the speculation of Plotinus: that mysterious entity, or non-entity, of matter, remains as elusive to modern physics as to the metaphysics of antiquity. Minerva too 'fabricated the variegated veil of nature, from that wisdom and virtue of which she is the presiding deity'. Her web is described by Ovid in his *Metamorphoses* in the story of the impious Arachne, changed into that lowly spinner, the spider. And Blake would have known also Spenser's figure of 'Great Dame Nature', herself a composite of all those earlier accounts of the veiled goddess:

> Then forth issewed (great goddess) great dame *Nature*,

> With goodly port and gracious Maiesty;
> Being far greater and more tall of stature
> Then any of the gods or Powers on hie:
> Yet certes by her face and physnomy,
> Whether she man or woman inly were,
> That could not any creature well descry:
> For with a veile that wimpled every where,
> Her head and face was hid, that mote to none appeare.
> (*Faery Queene* Book VII, Canto VII, V)

With the spreading influence of materialist thought in the modern West, Nature's beautiful veil becomes dark and opaque; Blake writes:

> I turn my eyes to the Schools & Universities of Europe
> And there behold the Loom of Locke, whose woof rages dire
> Wash'd by the water-wheels of Newton: black the cloth
> In heavy wreathes folds over every Nation (K636)

Vala's veil thus becomes 'a Law, a Terror & a Curse' as the so-called 'laws of nature' replace the knowledge of spiritual causes: 'Thund'ring the Veil rushes from his [Albion's] hand, Vegetating Knot by Knot, Day by Day, Night by Night.' (K648) As the black veil of natural appearances darkens, Albion's cities realize the nightmare of a materialist civilization, devoid of spiritual light:

> Till Norwood & Finchley & Blackheath & Hounslow cover'd
> the whole Earth.
> This is the Net & Veil of Vala among the Souls of the Dead
> (K671)

– of the spiritually dead: Blake knew of no other death. The veil of Vala ensnares the souls of those who have sunk into the waters of matter, ensnared by the seeming substantiality of appearances:

> For the Veil of Vala, which Albion cast into the Atlantic Deep
> To catch the Souls of the Dead, began to Vegetate & Petrify

Around the Earth of Albion among the Roots of his Tree.
(K691)

Yet Blake saw hope in the very beauty of the veil of natural appearances – the image of a divine order. And do we not indeed see in the study of the intricate and beautiful order of the natural sciences a possible way of return from the brink of chaos? Can the contemplation of the ordered beauty of nature itself make the veil of *maya* less black and dense? So Blake seemed to believe when he wrote:

Thus in process of time it became the beautiful Mundane Shell,
The Habitation of the Spectres of the Dead, & the Place
Of Redemption & of awaking again into Eternity (K691)

The veil, like the Indian *maya*, is a fluctuating texture of appearances, which now reflect, now conceal, the images of eternity:

According as they weave the little embryon nerves & veins,
The Eye, the little Nostrils & the delicate Tongue, & Ears
Of labyrinthine intricacy, so shall they fold the World,
That whatever is seen upon the Mundane Shell, the same
Be seen upon the Fluctuating Earth woven by the Sisters.
And sometimes the Earth shall roll in the Abyss & sometimes
Stand in the Center & sometimes stretch flat in the Expanse,
According to the will of the lovely Daughters of Albion;
Sometimes it shall assimilate with mighty Golgonooza,
Touching its summits, & sometimes divided roll apart.
As a beautiful veil, so these Females shall fold & unfold,
According to their will, the outside surface of the Earth,
An outside shadowy Surface superadded to the real Surface
Which is unchangeable for ever & ever (K728)

In Boehme's cosmology it is through corrupting the Nature-spirit that Satan distorts mankind's vision of reality; and Blake also speaks of 'that Veil which Satan puts between Eve & Adam'. The meaning is precise: Satan's veil is 'apprehensibility & comprehensibility' elevated into reality itself. As Satan is 'the mind of the natural frame', so 'Jesus, the Imagination' alone is able to rend the veil. Therefore Los, the Time-spirit, prays: 'Arise, O Lord, & rend the Veil!' Maya is 'a veil the Saviour born & dying rends'. In *The Gates of Paradise* this act of redemption is described. The goddess appears in her sinister aspect:

> Round her snowy Whirlwinds roar'd,
> Freezing her Veil, the Mundane Shell. (K770)

Because the Incarnation is an eternal event which takes place in every human birth, the poet can write: 'I rent the Veil where the Dead dwell'. (K770) This rending has something of the awful significance of the rending of the Veil of the Temple at the time of the Crucifixion.

Those who see in the history of ideas a design rather than a series of coincidences may reflect on the fact that the works of Plato, of Plotinus and the other Neoplatonists were translated into English by Thomas Taylor in the same years in which Sir William Jones and his circle (associated in the Proceedings of the Calcutta Society) were engaged in the translation of certain Indian scriptures. One may say that the time was ripe, the ground prepared, for the first impact of Indian thought upon the English-speaking world. Jones himself saw the *Vedas* in the context of the Platonic tradition and of Berkeley's philosophy, and wrote:

> The fundamental tenet of the *Vedanti* school . . . consisted, not in denying the existence of matter, that is, of solidity, impenetrability, and extended figure (to deny which would be lunacy), but, in correcting the popular notion of it, and in contending, that it has no essence independent of mental perception, that existence and perceptibility are convertible terms, that external appearances and sensations are illusory,

> and would vanish into nothing, if the divine energy, which alone sustains them, were suspended for a moment; an opinion which *Epicharmus* and *Plato* seem to have adopted, and which has been maintained in the present century with great elegance, but with little publick applause.
>
> ('On the Philosophy of the Asiaticks', *Asiatick Researches* IV: 171–2. *Works* III p.229 & f.)

He was referring of course to Berkeley.

Jones wrote of the concept of *maya*:

> the inextricable difficulties attending the *vulgar notion of material substances*, concerning which 'We know this only, that we nothing know', induced many of the wisest among the Ancients, and some of the more enlightened among the Moderns, to believe that the whole Creation was rather an *energy* than a work, by which the Infinite Being, who is present at all times in all places, exhibits to the minds of his creatures a set of perceptions, like a wonderful picture or piece of musick, always varied, yet always uniform; so that all bodies and their qualities exist, indeed, to every wise and useful purpose, but exist only as far as they are *perceived*; a theory no less pious than sublime, and as different from any principle of Atheism, as the brightest sunshine differs from the blackest midnight. This *illusive operation* of the Deity the *Hindu* philosophers call MAYA, or Deception.
>
> (Introduction to *Hymn to Narayena. Works* XIII, p. 302)

Like Isis, Juno and the rest of the European veiled goddesses, Maya is described as the mother of universal nature:

> *Maya*, or, as the word is explained by some Hindu scholars, 'the first inclination of the Godhead to diversify himself (such is their phrase) by creating worlds', is feigned to be the mother of universal nature, and of all the inferior Gods . . .

> but the word MAYA, or *delusion*, has a more subtle and recondite sense in the *Vedanta* philosophy, where it signifies the system of *perceptions*, whether of secondary or primary qualities, which the Deity was believed by Epicharmus, Plato, and many truly pious men, to raise up by his omnipresent spirit in the minds of his creatures, but which had not, in their opinion, any existence independent of mind.
>
> (*Asiatick Researches* I: 223. see also *Works* III, p.322)

When in *The Marriage of Heaven and Hell* Blake wrote that 'the philosophy of the East taught the first principles of human perception', was he referring to the Vedanta metaphysics?

Sir William Jones might have written expressly for Blake his remarks upon the *Hymn to Narayena*, which he also adapted from Vedantic sources, for he applies its metaphysical distinctions to the Descartes-Locke-Berkeley theme of primary and secondary sensible qualities. In the same way as Berkeley, the Hindu philosophy sees all alike as *maya*; 'the *sixth* stanza ascribes the perception of *secondary* qualities by our *senses* to the immediate influence of MAYA: and the *seventh* imputes to her operation the *primary* qualities of *extension* and solidity' (op. cit.).

Like Blake's Vala, *maya* is personified as a goddess. The hymn itself opens with the story of how Maya becomes the object of the love of her father in terms that closely resemble both Boehme's account of the seduction of man by the Nature-spirit, and Blake's account of the Giant Albion's seduction by Vala:

> Brahm his own mind survey'd
> As mortal eyes (thus finite we compare
> With infinite) in smoothest mirrors gaze:
> Swift, at his look, a shape supremely fair
> Leap'd into being with a boundless blaze,
> That fifty suns might daze.
> Primeval MAYA was the Goddess nam'd,
> Who to her sire, with Love divine inflam'd,

A casket gave with rich *Ideas* fill'd,
From which his gorgeous universe he fram'd.

The casket of Maya, filled with 'rich *Ideas*', is, once more, to be compared with the Platonic tradition of the 'seminal reasons' bestowed upon the soul of Nature by Intellect. Again, as in the European myths we have considered, the symbol of the mirror – Blake's 'Vegetable Glass of Nature' – appears.

The hymn describes (like the Hebrew Genesis myth) the creation of the waters of matter, from which rises the world-egg (Blake's 'Mundane Shell'), from which hatches the demiurge Brahma, seated on a lotus-throne. But Brahma, the demiurge creator, is posterior to Maya and subject to the veiled goddess:

Full-gifted BRAHMA! Rapt in solemn thought
He stood, and round his eyes fire-darting threw:
But, while his viewless origin he sought,
One plain he saw of living waters blue,
Their spring nor saw nor knew.
Then, in his parent stalk again retir'd,
With restless pain for ages he inquired
What were his pow'rs, by whom, and why conferr'd.
With doubts perplex'd, with keen impatience fir'd
He rose, and rising heard
Th'unknown all-knowing Word
'BRAHMA! no more in vain research persist:
My veil thou canst not move – Go: bid all words exist'.

In the conclusion of the hymn which retains much of India's grandeur even in Sir William Jones's eighteenth-century verse:

Blue crystal vault, and elemental fires,
That in the'thereal fluid blaze and breathe;
Thou, tossing main, whose snaky branches wreathe
This pensile orb with intertwisted gyres:
Mountains whose radiant spires

Presumptuous rear their summits to the skies,
And blend their em'rald hue with sapphire light;
Smooth meads and lawns, that glow with varying dyes
Of dew-bespangled leaves and blossoms bright,
Hence! vanish from my sight:
Delusive Pictures! unsubstantial shows!
My soul absorb'd One only Being knows,
Of all perceptions One abundant source,
Whence ev'ry object ev'ry moment flows:
Suns hence derive their force,
Hence planet learn their course;
But suns and fading worlds I view no more:
God only I perceive: God only I adore.

Or, in the words of Blake: 'Thus Nature is a Vision of the Science of Elohim.' (K518)

In speaking of Traditional metaphysics, whose mythological language is also universal, we cannot say that, as with literary sources, there is a single precise answer in questions of indebtedness: rather there is, in Blake, an enrichment of meaning from many tributaries through which the single, universal vision has reached him. Gifted as he was in symbolic thought, he recognized in her many guises the veiled goddess, of whom traces are to be found in Platonic myths and Hermetic teachings of a body of thought totally developed only perhaps in India. How full the Indian tradition was Blake could hardly, at the end of the eighteenth century, have known; but it is certain that he at least glimpsed afar off the venerable tradition of the *Vedas*, in some degree reflected in his prophetic message to his own nation.

Mythologizing of Time in Blake's Prophetic Books

AT THE END of the eighteenth century Western thought was preoccupied with the natural order and the development of the natural sciences, in the belief, made the more credible by the inventions of technology, that these provide a full and sufficient account of the universe.

Blake totally rejected the scientific paradigm which situates the phenomenal world in space and time, within the dimensions of length, breadth, height and duration. On the contrary, he situates spaces, times, duration and all appearances within mind. Knowledge, as Blake clearly saw, is inseparable from a knower. Not 'matter' but Imagination is the primary reality, using the word in the sense of Jacob Boehme, the German theosophist whom he acknowledged as a Master, who wrote 'The beginning of all existence is nothing other than an imagination of the *ungrund*,' the *ungrund* being his term for Godhead, as an object unknowable.

Blake's rejection of materialism was total and uncompromising: existence is not in space but in mind, not in time but in the inexhaustible fecundity of forms within the Imagination. Man is not a natural body situated in time and space but immeasurable spirit. All times and spaces, all the numberless places and times of existence, have their being in universal Imagination. In this sense life is 'eternal' not through temporal duration but because being itself is not in time and space; the brief moment of the 'summer's play' of the little fly is a manifestation of immeasurable being, infinite in its least as in its greatest parts. Blake never changed his essential teaching, but in each successive work expanded and extended his picture – I would say 'clarified' but in terms of current materialism the symbolic and mythological terms in which Blake set forth a view of reality so totally at variance with current notions would hardly be called so.

Many themes and details of his works are traceable to his one-time friend Thomas Taylor the Platonist's writings and translations of the works of Plato, Plotinus, and other Neoplatonists; to the alchemical theosophy of Jacob Boehme; to Christian Cabbala, even to the *Bhagavad-Gita*. He had read many works of mythology, including Jacob Bryant's then famous *New System of Mythology*, an early essay in comparative mythology for which Blake as a young man engraved several plates. But while many details come from these and other works, Blake's system as a whole can only be understood in depth in the light of the eighteenth century Swedish visionary, Emanuel Swedenborg, of whose Church of the New Jerusalem, founded in London, Blake was an early attendant. As a young man Blake was a devoted reader of Swedenborg, whose works he studied and annotated.

Swedenborg was a distinguished scientist (Assessor of Minerals to the Swedish government) who in middle life experienced what he describes as an 'opening' of his inner worlds, and a total transformation of consciousness. Following this experience he wrote many volumes on the nature and inhabitants of these inner worlds, which continue to be regarded as fundamental texts by all concerned with psychical research. In *Heaven and Hell*, and *Wisdom of the Angels concerning Divine Love and Divine Wisdom*, which Blake possessed and annotated with close attention, Swedenborg expounds his essential teaching. Central to that teaching is the understanding that 'the Divine is not in space':

That the Divine, namely, God, is not in space, although the

> Divine is omnipresent and with every man in the world and with every angel in heaven [i.e. in the inner worlds] and with every spirit under heaven cannot be comprehended by a merely natural idea, but by a spiritual idea. It cannot be comprehended by a natural idea because there is space in that idea; for it is formed out of such things as are in the world, and in each and all of these things, which strike the eye, there is space. Everything great and small there is of Space; everything long, broad and high there is of Space; in short, every measure, figure and form there is of space. (DLW 7)

To this Blake comments in the margin 'What a natural idea is' – that is, spatial. Spaces of the inner worlds, Swedenborg goes on to say,

> appear similar to spaces in earth, and yet they are not spaces but appearances. Thus they are not fixed and settled as on earth; they can be lengthened and shortened; they can be changed and varied; and so because they cannot be determined by measure.

As with spaces, so with times:

> instead of spaces there are such things as have relation to states of love, and instead of times there are such things as have relation to states of wisdom. (70)

In his own *Marriage of Heaven and Hell* – a parody, commentary and criticism of Swedenborg's *Heaven and Hell* – Blake writes, 'The hours of folly are measur'd by the clock; but of wisdom no clock can measure.' (K151)

Swedenborg is mainly concerned with the worlds of discarnate spirits. These, he reports, can build up surroundings – houses and gardens, garments, paradises or stifling hells – instantaneously in accordance with their thoughts and states of love or wisdom. Spaces in nature are measurable and so is time; but in the inner worlds are not fixed but flexible, in accordance with changes of thought or mood. Discarnate spirits, Swedenborg reports, can build up thought-forms in an instant. We in the twentieth century can hardly fail to draw comparison with dreams whose times and spaces are likewise 'correspondences' (to use Swedenborg's term) to states of mind. These worlds of fluctuating appearances and shifting landscapes belong also to popular folklore concerning 'fairies' and other inhabitants of mental worlds, in all countries. W.B. Yeats, Blake's first editor and greatest disciple, was likewise a follower of Swedenborg, and in an important paper entitled 'Swedenborg, Mediums and the Desolate Places' draws a comparison between the 'other-world' of Celtic folk tradition, where likewise houses and cattle, garments and landscapes are built up in an instant, as with Swedenborg's spirit-worlds.

Blake, who adopted Swedenborg's hierarchy of inner and higher worlds and their unlimited creativity in 'correspondence' with mental states and thoughts, was not greatly concerned with an after-life, but rather with the structure of the inner worlds and the infinite creativity of the Imagination. Although this term Blake took not from Swedenborg but from Boehme, Swedenborg's sublime vision of the Divine-Human, the many-in-one and one-in-many which for him made up the supreme Person of the 'heavens' or inner worlds, Blake made his own. Life, as Blake understood it through Swedenborg's astonishing vision of the whole of the 'heavens' as the body of 'One Man', the 'Divine Humanity' is in its nature immortal, eternal, infinite and indivisible whether in the ephemeral fly or minute flower or grain of sand, or in the entire universe. Not a divisible universe of space-time, but an infinite universe of indivisible being, life, boundless and self-delighting, in the universal Body of the Divine Human which is 'not in space' and neither large nor small.

In the material world of 'objects' measurement, quantification, is the sole means of knowledge. In the world of immeasurable life, moods and meanings, states of being, heavens and hells, paradises and dreams, cannot be quantified. Since states of being presume a Person who experiences, the inner worlds have at all times been populous with gods and angels, demons and fairy people, embodiments and enactors of thoughts and moods of a mental universe. These are immeasurable, and all attempts to quantify meaning and being itself are futile, since the inner universe is by its nature not subject to quantification, as Swedenborg and Blake understood. In that world knowledge is a mode of being. Such is the world of the Imagination, and the arts are the native language not of the mortal world but of the soul's immortal, immeasurable kingdom.

Swedenborg describes this inner universe as the domain of the divine Love and the divine Wisdom, the twofold essence of life in its infinite variety. But Swedenborg's decidedly prosaic conversations with discarnate human spirits cannot be said to constitute a mythology. Blake, however, from the outset imagined mythologically, his poetic universe is populous with ephemeral spirits of flower and insect, energies of the human soul, transient or abiding, as are the gods of traditional pantheons. His inner worlds, throughout his writings, become ever more complex and rich in enactments, conflicts and wars and reconciliations of the energies and moods of life.

No other poet has created, from their living source, a full pantheon of gods and their *shaktis* or 'emanations', the uncurbed energies of life in conflict or in harmony. Beyond that universe of the Imagination lies the unknowable; and Blake writes of his four 'mighty ones' of the human drama:

> What are the Natures of those Living Creatures the Heav'nly
> Father only Knoweth.
> No Individual knoweth nor can know in all Eternity. (K264)

We may recall a famous text from the Vedas,

> Who verily knows, and who can here declare it,
> Whence it was born, and whence comes this creation?

The gods are later than this world's production,
Who knows, then, whence it first came into being?.
(tr. Max Müller)

The quantitative thought of the natural sciences has no need of pantheons. It deals in 'objects', which can be observed and measured, but are devoid of the qualities and attributes, meanings and moods, of life. But, as C.G. Jung has rediscovered in this century, these living Persons nevertheless continue to populate our inner universe. They have not gone away. We meet them in our dreams. Blake's Four Zoas, their acts and aspects, have become real and familiar to many, not as figments of fancy, but as a recognizable pantheon of the English collective psyche: blind Urizen poring over his books of the Law; fiery Orc chained to his rock; Vala, goddess of nature, with her veil; Los, the 'eternal prophet' creating and destroying the productions of Time on his anvil, in the 'furnaces of affliction'. Their natures and acts are the inner causes of the outer events of personal and national history, political, military, ideological. Quantification is inapplicable to the inner worlds of which symbol and myth are the appropriate terms. There cannot in this sense ever be a 'science' of mental states, in their nature immeasurable.

Blake, in an early work *The Marriage of Heaven and Hell*, takes up a mythological quarrel with the author of *Paradise Lost*. He accuses Milton of having made Reason his Messiah, casting the forces of energy, or desire, into hell. But this history, says Blake, 'has been adopted by both parties'. 'It indeed appear'd to Reason as if Desire was cast out; but the Devil's account is, that the Messiah fell, & formed a heaven of what he stole from the Abyss'. (K150). Reason's world is only a 'stolen' portion of the inexhaustible universe of the Imagination.

For Blake it is Urizen, the systematizing rational mind who imposes on the unbounded energies of life a structure based on the observations of the senses. The *Book of Urizen* recapitulates the

Miltonic story of the Creation, according to 'the Devil's account' of how the Messiah or Reason 'form'd a heaven of what he stole from the Abyss'. What he 'stole' was, precisely, a world confined within the bounds of space and time—length, breadth, height and duration. Blake begins his creation-myth by a reference to the Newtonian system and its natural cosmology:

> Earth was not: nor globes of attraction;
> The will of the Immortal expanded
> Or contracted his all flexible senses;
> Death was not, but eternal life sprung. (K223)

It is natural reason who creates the world of space and time, and Blake asks,

> . . . what Demon
> Hath form'd this abominable void,
> This soul-shudd'ring vacuum? (K222)

Milton's

> Immutable, Eternal, Infinite,
> Eternal King; thee Author of all being,
> Fountain of Light, thyself invisible
> . . .
> Thron'd inaccessible

—is, for Blake 'That solitary one in Immensity', Urizen, 'the mind of the natural frame'. This separation of earth as 'a black globe', 'self-balanced', like Milton's earth that 'self-balanc'd on her Center hung' Blake saw as the separation of a finite material universe from life itself.

Urizen's creation is a limitation imposed, and that limitation is a binding, not of Nature but of the Eternal Mind—Urizen himself. Life is bounded and limited within a mortal body, the eternal mind shut within the 'cavern' of the skull—Plato's Cave here understood as the prison in which 'man has closed himself up, till he sees all things thro' narrow chinks of his cavern' – the five senses. (K154) As for the eternal world of life, it is excluded from Urizen's natural creation; and the 'inhabitants' of eternity are thrown into fury and sorrow:

> All the myriads of Eternity,
> All the visions & joy of life
> Roll like a sea around him,
> Except what his little orbs
> Of sight by degrees unfold.
>
> And now his eternal life
> Like a dream was obliterated. (K230)

The seven days of Urizen's labours of creation were the seven stages of the binding and circumscribing of the Eternal Mind:

> Six days they shrunk up from existence,
> And on the seventh day they rested,
> And they bless'd the seventh day, in sick hope
> And forgot their eternal life. (K236)

The 'seventh day' represents 'the limit of contraction' of eternal into temporal life through the narrowing perceptions of mankind. It was Boehme who declared that creation, in limiting the 'Fall', 'is an act of mercy'.

Clear to Blake, but even now largely incomprehensible to the Western mind conditioned by that same 'binding' Blake describes not less than three times in his Prophetic Books, such was his urgency to communicate the true situation. Urizen's 'black globe' is not a creation *ex nihilo*, the created world is 'the Void Outside of Existence which if enter'd into / Becomes a Womb' (K534) and into this 'womb' souls are generated, to become subjected to the conditions of a material existence, outside eternity. Plato too understood this world to be a 'cave closed off from the universe'.

As Urizen, 'Aged Ignorance', is known by the books he continually writes, the stone Tables of the Law, and his purblindness (sometimes represented by spectacles without which he cannot see, as he pursues his unending labours of codifying and making new laws to contain the uncurbed energies of life,) so Los, in the Book of Urizen, is personified as the forger of Time at his Furnaces, with the beat of his hammer he forges on his anvil the chains of Time to contain Urizen's dark sorrowful world within bounds, '. . . forging chains new & new, Numb'ring with links hours, days & years'. (K227) The 'infinite Fires' of eternity 'flow down in the winds' (of Inspiration) from the eternal worlds into Los's 'furnaces of affliction'. Blake's Prophet of Eternity who with his rhythmic hammer-blows both forges and destroys the productions of Time, may surely be compared to the Lord Shiva whose rhythmic dance in the guise of Time destroys all generated forms. Whatever can be created can be destroyed, for the duration of Urizen's material world 'outside existence' is finite, and its nature is illusory. Like Shiva, Los is also a phallic god; Space (Enitharmon) and Time (Los) are the parents of souls drawn down into the world of generation 'The Male is a Furnace of beryll; and the Female is a golden Loom.' (K623) The rhythm of Los's hammer as, like Shiva, he generates and destroys the productions of Time, is the heart-beat.

The fallacy of materialist thought is to take the part—the material order—for the whole. Swedenborg, in common with other traditional cosmologies, describes a fourfold hierarchy of worlds, as does Blake, whose terms, 'Eden', 'Beulah' and, the world of generation, point to Swedenborg as his immediate source:

> Now I a fourfold vision see,
> And a fourfold vision is given to me
> 'Tis fourfold in my supreme delight
> And threefold in soft Beulah's night
> And twofold Always. May God us keep
> From Single vision and Newton's sleep! (K818)

Los alone, with his 'emanation' Enitharmon, is born (in the words of Wordsworth's 'Ode on the Intimations of Immortality') 'not in entire forgetfulness'. As the agents of Time and Space, Los and Enitharmon 'descend' into generation from eternity by way of an inter-world Blake names 'Beulah'. 'Beulah' is a Biblical symbol of the state of marriage (also used by Bunyan in *Pilgrim's Progress*) taken from Isaiah LXII:4, 'The land shall be called Beulah: for the Lord delighteth in thee, and thy land shall be married'. Blake's Beulah is an amorous Paradisal state where dream-spaces are not prisons, as in Urizen's 'world of rocky destiny', but shelters, refuges, not shut off from higher worlds. Here, as in dreams – as in Swedenborg's 'heavens' – times and spaces are not fixed and dead, but expansive, reflecting the 'states' of the dreamers:

> There is from Great Eternity a mild & pleasant rest
> Nam'd Beulah, a soft Moony Universe, feminine, lovely,
> Pure, mild & Gentle, given in Mercy to those who sleep,
> Eternally created by the Lamb of God around,
> On all sides, within & without the Universal Man.
> The Daughters of Beulah follow sleepers in all their Dreams,
> Creating Spaces, lest they fall into Eternal Death.

Urizen's time-world – his 'Circle of Destiny' – is in reality only one of the dream-spaces of Beulah:

> The Circle of Destiny complete they gave it a Space,
> And nam'd the space Ulro, & brooded over it in care & love.
>
> (K266–7)

In Urizen's world the sheltering dream-spaces become 'deadly sleep', even death itself – spiritual death that is – and Beulah's 'spaces' therefore become 'graves', 'funeral urns', 'funeral arks'; but still with the hope of resurrection. Therefore the Daughters of Beulah 'the Eternal Promise'

> . . . wrote on all their tombs & pillars, & on every Urn

These words: 'If ye will believe, your Brother shall rise again'
In golden letters ornamented with sweet labours of Love,
Waiting with patience for the fulfilment of the Promise Divine.
(K340)

At the end of *Jerusalem*, Blake's last Prophetic Book, the promise is fulfilled and humanity awakes from the mortal dream – 'All was a Vision, all a Dream' (K744) with no more substantiality than Shakespeare's 'cloud-capped towers'. All the heavens and hells of mortal life are 'States that are not, but ah! seem to be!' (K522) In his description of his great composition, *A Vision of the Last Judgment*, on which he was working at the end of his life, Blake again describes the lives of this world as dreams:

> ... I do not consider either the Just or the Wicked to be in a Supreme State, but to be every one of them States of Sleep which the Soul may fall into in its deadly dreams of Good & Evil when it leaves Paradise following the Serpent. (K614)

Again we see Blake reaching an insight comparable to Far-Eastern mythologies of, for example, the Buddhist wheel of states of existence. Beulah is the soul's universe, situated, in the hierarchy of 'worlds', between the natural and the spiritual orders. Only the Imagination is 'not a state' but, in Blake's words, 'the Human Existence itself'. (K522)

The Circle of Destiny, then, is the time-world, a dream-space whose duration of six thousand years is a finite space created in Beulah, into which Los and Enitharmon – Time and Space – are born, and their children; Blake mythologises as follows:

Then Eno, a daughter of Beulah, took a Moment of Time
And drew it out to seven thousand years with much care & affliction
And many tears, & in every year made windows into Eden.
She also took an atom of space & opened its centre
Into Infinitude & ornamented it with wondrous art.

> Astonish'd sat her sisters of Beulah to see her soft affection
> To Enion & her children . . . (K270)

– that is, Los and Enitharmon, regents of Time and Space.

Beulah, the world of the soul, receives its dreams from Imagination itself. In *Jerusalem* Blake again writes of these 'spaces':

> She (the female) Creates at her will a little moony night &
> silence
> With Spaces of sweet gardens & a tent of elegant beauty,
> Closed in by a sandy desart & a night of stars shining
> And a little tender moon & hovering angels on the wing;
> And the Male gives a Time & Revolution to her Space
> Till the time of love is passed in ever varying delights.
> For All Things Exist in the Human Imagination,
> And thence in Beulah they are stolen in secret amorous theft.
> (K707)

In *Jerusalem* Blake repeats the theme of the creation of the time-world by 'an Aged Pensive Woman' here named not Eno but Erin:

> With awful hands she took
> A Moment of Time, drawing it out with many tears & afflictions,
> And many sorrows . . .
> Into a Rainbow of jewels & gold . . .
> Eight thousand and five hundred years
> In its extension. Every two hundred years it has a door into Eden.
> She also took an Atom of Space, with dire pain opening it a Center
> Into Beulah. (K678)

'Erin's lovely bow' is the vision of the eternal world of the Imagination whose 'windows' and 'doors' open from the time-world into timeless heavens. Every two hundred years, or, as in the earlier account, every year, suggests great poetic or prophetic visions; but elsewhere Blake tells of 'a moment in each day' that communicates with ever present eternity:

> There is a Moment in each Day, that Satan cannot find
> Nor can his Watch Fiends find it; but the Industrious find
> This Moment & it multiply, when it once is found
> It renovates every Moment of the Day if rightly placed.
>
> (K526)

Such is the artist's moment of inspiration. The timeless moment is infinite; eternity is whole and indivisible, Swedenborg taught, in the least as in the greatest things.

In a passage of great beauty Blake builds the cloud-capped towers of the dream of mortal life:

> . . . the Sons of Los built Moments & Minutes & Hours
> And Days & Months & Years & Ages & Periods, wondrous buildings;
> And every Moment has a Couch of gold for soft repose
> (A Moment equals a pulsation of the artery),
> And between every two Moments stands a Daughter of Beulah
> To feed the Sleepers on their Couches with maternal care.
> And every Minute has an azure Tent with silken Veils:
> And every Hour has a bright golden Gate carved with skill:
> And every Day & Night has Walls of brass & Gates of adamant,
> Shining like precious Stones & ornamented with appropriate signs:
> And every Month a silver paved Terrace builded high:
> And every Year invulnerable Barriers with high Towers:
> And every Age is Moated deep with Bridges of silver & gold:
> And every Seven Ages is Incircled with a Flaming Fire.
> Now Seven Ages is amounting to Two Hundred Years.
> Each has its Guard, each Moment, Minute, Hour, Day, Month & Year.
> All are the work of Fairy hands of the Four Elements:

The Guard are Angels of Providence on duty evermore.
Every Time less than a pulsation of the artery
Is equal in its period & value to Six Thousand Years,
For in this period the Poet's Work is Done, and all the Great
Events of Time start forth & are conceiv'd in such a Period,
Within a Moment, a Pulsation of the Artery. (K516)

There follows an equally eloquent account of the creation of Space which concludes in a like manner:

every Space larger than a red Globule of Man's blood
Is visionary: and is created by the Hammer of Los;
And every Space smaller than a Globule of Man's blood opens
Into Eternity of which this vegetable Earth is but a shadow.
The red Globule is the unwearied Sun by Los created
To measure Time and Space to Mortal Man every morning.
(K516–7)

The First Book of *Milton* from which these magnificent passages setting forth Blake's apologia for the Imagination as the creator of worlds are taken concludes with the words,

Such is the World of Los, the labour of six thousand years.
Thus Nature is a Vision of the Science of the Elohim. (K518)

—the seven creator-spirits of God, the fountain-spirits of Jacob Boehme, which become the Seven Furnaces of Los the Eternal Prophet—the 'Furnaces of Affliction' which become fountains once more in the renewal of humanity, as told in the concluding passages of Jerusalem; there is clearly an allusion to Boehme's 'fontal spirits' in this otherwise inexplicable transformation as the Giant Albion awakes:

So Albion . . . threw himself into the Furnaces of affliction.
All was a Vision, all a Dream: the Furnaces became
Fountains of Living Waters flowing from the Humanity Divine.
(K744)

The theme of the 'opening of the centres of the birth of life' Blake certainly borrowed from the profound cosmological insights of Boehme, who uses the image very frequently. This 'infinite centre' may be compared to the concept of 'zero' (as developed in India), which introduces into the unending repetition of the series of numbers another dimension. In terms of Western materialist science this has no meaning; and thus we find Blake writing that in Satan's Kingdom'—that is, the natural world as a self-contained system—the centre is 'a white dot' (K659) a mere point in space. The 'infinite centres' of the birth of life, by contrast, open into eternity, out of space and time altogether. In the Centre there is God; as Boehme writes, 'Where do you want to look for God? In the deep above the stars? There you will not find Him. Look in your heart, in the centre of the birth of your life—there you will find Him.' (*Three Principles of the Divine Essence* 4:8) Commenting on this concept, Peter Malekin points out that 'Centre' is 'a technical term in Boehme for the source, origin, or inner principle from which something flows into outer manifest existence (the outermost level of existence being the physical world which flows out of, or emanates from the inner worlds.)'* And so with Blake:

'The Vegetative Universe opens like a flower from the Earth's
center
In which is Eternity. It expands in Stars to the Mundane Shell
And there it meets Eternity again, both within and without.
And the abstract Voids between the Stars are the Satanic
Wheels (K633)

—the astronomical revolutions as conceived in the materialist Newtonian cosmology.

Blake has a particular love for images of the minute; the little winged fly, the tiny flowers of the meadow-sweet and the wild

* Jacob Boehme, *The Key and Other Writings* translated by Peter Malekin, (Durham, 1988) p.12.

thyme 'Los's messenger to Eden'. Here indeed the word 'thyme' ('time') is also a metaphor evoking the timeless moment which opens into eternity. The flowers

> . . . put forth their precious Odours,
> And none can tell how from so small a centre comes such sweets,
> Forgetting that within that Centre Eternity expands
> Its ever during doors. (K520)

Such is the depth and height of spiritual understanding that Blake could express with such simplicity in his familiar lines

> To see a World in a Grain of Sand
> And a Heaven in a Wild Flower,
> Hold Infinity in the palm of your hand
> And Eternity in an hour. (K431)

The lark who heralds morning draws his inspiration from that same 'infinite centre' so that 'nature' with all its splendour must pay homage to the source which is not to be found in nature but in eternity:

> His little throat labours with inspiration; every feather
> On throat & breast & wings vibrates with the effluence Divine.
> All Nature listens silent to him, & the awful Sun
> Stands still upon the Mountain looking on this little Bird
> With eyes of soft humility & wonder, love & awe. (K520)

To return to Los and Enitharmon, those twin babes new-born into 'the moony spaces of Eno', into Beulah, that inter-world between Time and Eternity. At first they retain their imaginative power, as in Swedenborg's 'heavens', over times and spaces, still flexible to thought:

> Nine Times they liv'd among the forests, feeding on sweet fruits,
> And nine bright Spaces wander'd, weaving mazes of delight.
> . . .

He could controll the times & seasons, & the days & years.
She could controll the spaces, regions, desart, flood & forest.

(K270–1)

Swedenborg's power of controlling times and spaces is confined to discarnate spirits but for Blake it belongs to the prophetic genius, whose link with the Imagination has never been severed. It is the poet's gift to experience the 'state' of eternity in an hour:

For Los & Enitharmon walk'd forth on the dewy Earth
Contracting or expanding their all flexible senses
At will to murmur in the flowers small as the honey bee,
At will to stretch across the heavens or step from star to star.
Or standing on the Earth erect or on the stormy waves
Driving the storms before them, or delighting in sunny beams
While round their heads the Elemental Gods kept harmony.

(K288)

Therefore, Blake admonishes,

Let the Human Organs be kept in their perfect Integrity,
At will Contracting into Worms or Expanding into Gods

. . .

. . . for tho' we sit down within
The plowed furrow, list'ning to the weeping clods till we
Contract or Expand Space at will, or if we raise ourselves
Upon the chariots of the morning, Contracting or Expanding
Time,
Every one knows we are One Family, One Man blessed for ever.

(K686–7)

The 'One Man' is the universal Imagination, the One of whom the many are manifestations, while yet remaining within the single Divine Body, at once many and one.

This figure of the Divine Humanity is very close to Swedenborg's 'Grand Man' of the heavens (or inner worlds) in whose single body all the living are contained. From Swedenborg also comes the concept of flexible times and spaces; indeed this is one of Swedenborg's leading ideas. In the natural world, Swedenborg writes, since 'Spaces of Nature are not appearances of Spaces according to States of Life, as in the Spiritual World they also may be called dead' (*Divine Love and Wisdom of the Angels* para. 160). When Urizen, the reasoner, supplants the Imagination and declares himself supreme god, Los, the Time-spirit, falls under his tyranny: 'Now fix'd into one stedfast bulk his features stonify', while

> Enitharmon stretched on the *dreary* earth.
> Felt her immortal limbs freeze, stiffening, pale, inflexible.
> His feet shrunk with'ring from the deep, shrinking & with-
> ering,
> And Enitharmon shrunk up, all their fibres with'ring beneath,
> As plants wither'd by winter, leaves & stems & roots decaying
> Melt into thin air . . .
> So Los & Enitharmon,
> Shrunk into fixed space, stood trembling on a Rocky cliff,
> Yet mighty bulk & majesty & beauty remain'd, but unexpansive.
> . . .
> Their senses unexpansive in one stedfast bulk remain. (K305)

Throughout his writings, Blake's landscape obeys the Swedenborgian law of 'correspondence', the '*dreary* earth' and 'Rocky Cliff' contrasting with the bee in the flowers, the sunny beams and moving waters of the world of Imagination. As with Los and Enitharmon, so with the living creatures of the Ulro; for all creatures are, like men, living spirits, boundless and expansive. Blake asks

> Seest thou the little winged fly, smaller than a grain of sand?
> It has a heart like thee, a brain open to heaven & hell,
> Withinside wondrous & expansive, its gates are not clos'd:

I hope thine are not: hence it clothes itself in rich array:
Hence thou art cloth'd with human beauty, O thou mortal man.

The passage continues with an allusion to natural space which, in contrast with the eternity within, does not reveal God. The allusion to Boehme's contrasting of 'the deeps above the stars' and the infinity within the heart is clearly present:

Seek not thy heavenly father then beyond the skies,
There Chaos dwells & Ancient Night (K502)

Blake's fly is a Swedenborgian fly, its rich array corresponding with its nature, as all spirits create for themselves their garments, surroundings and landscapes in accordance with their states of Love and Wisdom. But as the perceptive organs close to the eternal worlds, so nature comes to seem fixed and dead:

If Perceptive Organs vary, Objects of Perception seem to vary:
If the Perceptive Organs close, their Objects seem to close also.
'Consider this, O Mortal Man, O worm of sixty winters,' said Los.
(K661)

The closed world is in reality the closed consciousness of 'the worm of sixty winters'. To Blake this was a grievous, appalling limitation of the infinite senses of humanity, in a narrowed world:

How are the Beasts & Birds & Fishes & Plants & Minerals
Here fix'd into a frozen bulk subject to decay & death?
Those Visions of Human Life & Shadows of Wisdom &
Knowledge
Are here frozen into unexpansive deadly destroying terrors
(K525)

Los is 'the Eternal Prophet' 'inspired' by the God within. Los and Enitharmon are therefore able to build, in the Ulro, the 'City of Golgonooza', the 'spiritual fourfold London' whose inhabitants –

the 'sons' and 'daughters' of Los and Enitharmon his *Shakti*, build according to the archetype of the eternal world of the Imagination. Thus a great family comes into being by whose labours the time-world is regenerated.

Satan also is born into the time-world and is therefore a 'son' of Los and Enitharmon. The true Satan, according to Blake, is not the Miltonic Satan of energy and desire, but the Miltonic Messiah of Reason – Blake's Urizen. Blake is here writing with specific reference to the materialist domination of Western thought in his own time and place and the current ideologies whose domination he deplored, and denounced. To this day Bacon and Newton remain culture-heroes of the English nation, and not the visionaries Whitfield and Wesley who were 'witnesses', as was St. Teresa of Avila and the French 'quietist' Fénelon, whom Blake saw as proclaiming the inner universe as against the institutional Churches. But above all the enemy Blake challenged was the mechanistic science whose spectacular rise he was witnessing, and whose authority has remained into our own century. Indeed only in this century has the force of Blake's challenge to the scientific pretention to be final arbiter of truth (tacitly acknowledged by the 'deism' of 'natural religion' of the churches, which rejected revelation from an inner invisible source) begun to be recognized. Los, as the Time-spirit into whose world Satan – Urizen – is born in the guise of the materialist science, precisely identifies the mentality Blake sets out to challenge:

> O Satan, my youngest born, art thou not Prince of the Starry
> Hosts
> And of the Wheels of Heaven, to turn the Mills day & night?
> Art thou not Newton's Pantocrator, weaving the Woof of
> Locke?
> To Mortals thy Mills seem every thing. (K483)

The space-time world is created to contain and circumscribe Satan, whose nature is here more precisely defined, as 'the mind of the natural frame'. Here it is Enitharmon herself who from the 'moony' interworld of Beulah, forms the Ulro, the space-time world of six thousand years. It is, again, a dream-space, one of 'the deadly dreams the soul falls into when it leaves Eden', 'drawn out', as in the earlier accounts, with 'many tears'. In *Milton* Enitharmon herself is the sorrower:

> Oft Enitharmon enter'd weeping into the Space, there appearing
> An aged Woman raving along the Streets . . .
> . . . then she returned to Los, weary, frighted as from dreams.
> (K490)

The 'spaces' of Beulah are called 'female spaces' since the space 'becomes a womb' through which souls are generated into this world. Enitharmon creates the time-world not for Satan alone, but to contain the eternal contraries, here depicted as Satan, and Michael, leader of the heavenly hosts. Blake is here returning to his earlier theme of *The Marriage of Heaven and Hell.* This 'space' is called a 'lunar' space, again with reference to the feminine 'moony night' of Beulah, through which souls 'descend' from eternity into the world of generation:

> The nature of a Female Space is this: it shrinks the Organs
> Of Life till they become Finite & Itself seems Infinite.
> And Satan vibrated in the immensity of the Space, Limited
> To those without, but Infinite to those within. (K490–1)

This space is now called 'Canaan', the 'promised land' into which in course of time the Divine Humanity, 'Jesus the Imagination' will be born as the 'saviour'. It is also, by implication, Plato's cave,

> . . . 'a vast Concave Earth'
> Enlarg'd into dimension and deform'd into indefinite space
> In Twenty-seven Heavens & all their Hells, with Chaos
> And Ancient Night & Purgatory. It is a cavernous Earth

> Of labyrinthine intricacy, twenty-seven-folds of opakeness,
> And finishes where the lark mounts. (K498)

These lines are compact with resonances and allusions to Blake's multiple sources. The number twenty-seven alludes to Swedenborg who described twenty-seven 'churches' or periods, between the creation and the end of the time-world. Chaos and Ancient Night are Miltonic, while Purgatory alludes to Dante. Blake's horrendous vision is history itself, 'Satan's Seat' is in this world; which in another passage Blake calls 'The Lost Traveller's dream under the hill' – Dante's Mountain of Purgatory which stands over the hells. These end 'where the Lark mounts' – the bird that for so many English poets, including Milton himself, embodies poetic Inspiration which rises above the deadly dreams of mortal life we experience as history.

Consistent with the symbol of the singing soaring Lark is yet another symbolic attribution of 'Canaan' which becomes 'the Mundane Shell', the world-egg, a world-wide symbol, doubtless known to Blake from the Orphic mythology. As an apprentice engraver he had worked on the illustrations of Jacob Bryant's *New System of Mythology* in which the Orphic egg is represented, in one illustration, surmounted by a crescent moon; just as Enitharmon, in creating the 'space' for 'Satan & Michael & for the poor infected' 'clos'd it with a tender Moon' (K489), as is indeed appropriate to the 'moony spaces' of Beulah which through the moon also become a measure of Time. Such symbolic discourse is densely concentrated with both natural and cultural allusions and meanings which could scarcely be brought together by discursive presentation, but which are the proper language of myth. Blake used this language of the Imagination – a language of images – with a natural mastery only to be paralleled in traditional mythologies.

Thus the 'female space' of Canaan, the six thousand years of history, becomes the 'mundane egg' from which in course of time the Divine Humanity will emerge like a bird from its shell. Bird and butterfly are both familiar classical emblems of the immortal soul 'hatched' from the mortal body. In other versions of the 'spaces' of Beulah, these are described as 'funeral urns' or 'arks' which contain the Holy of Holies. For Blake 'Man is the Ark of God' – or as the 'womb' into which the Divine Humanity enters the world of generation. As the Mundane Shell, the emphasis of this multiple symbol is on the final act of the 'hatching' of immortal souls whose 'wings' have grown which will carry them back to their native country. That the time-world ends 'where the Lark mounts' already suggests the hatching of the living spirits from the world-egg; wings being also Plato's symbol of spiritual aspiration. There is, besides, in a series of small emblems entitled *The Gates of Paradise*, one which depicts a winged infant springing from between the halves of a broken shell, with the words beneath 'At length for hatching ripe he breaks the shell'. The parents of generated souls, Los and Enitharmon (Time and Space) as they labour in the time-world within the Mundane Shell can hear 'the family of Eden', spirits of the eternal world, as they await the hour of 'hatching':

> Seven mornings Los heard them, as the poor bird within the
> shell
> Hears the impatient parent bird, and Enitharmon heard them
> But saw them not, for the blue Mundane Shell inclos'd them in.
> (K504)

The end of the time-world is a return to imaginative consciousness, and is the work of Los, the Eternal Prophet. Blake, as the poet who throughout his life, proclaimed the doctrine of the Imagination, identifies himself with Los: 'and Los behind me stood, a terrible flaming sun',

> . . . but he kissed me and wish'd me health,
> And I became One Man with him arising in my strength.
> 'Twas too late now to recede. Los had enter'd into my soul:

His terrors now possess'd me whole! I arose in fury & strength.
(K505)

Since the time-world has been illusory, Los proclaims that at the end of Time all exists in the timeless world of Imagination;

I am that Shadowy Prophet who Six Thousand Years ago
Fell from my station in the Eternal bosom. Six Thousand Years
Are finish'd. I return! both Time & Space obey my will.
I in Six Thousand Years walk up and down; for not one Moment
Of Time is lost, nor one Event of Space unpermanent,
But all remain; every fabric of Six Thousand Years
Remains permanent, tho' on the Earth where Satan
Fell and was cut off, all things vanish and are seen no more,
They vanish not from me & mine, we guard them first & last.
The generations of men run on the tide of Time
But leave their destin'd lineaments permanent for ever & ever.
(K505)

All is permanent in the timeless order of the Imagination; or as Yeats writes, 'All things remain in God'. Or we may recall Rilke's perception in the ninth Duino Elegy:

These things that live on departure
Understand when you praise them: fleeting, they look for rescue
Through something in us, the most fleeting of all. Want us
To change them entirely, within our invisible hearts, into –
Oh endlessly – into ourselves. Whosoever we are.
(Translated by J.B. Leishman & Stephen Spender)

Blake may have been premature in his prophecy that the six thousand years of the time-world is ended but that he was both prophet and agent of a New Age of the supremacy of Imagination who can doubt? The world of mortality is illusory, 'a delusion of Ulro', real existence is in the Imagination: all living beings carry their 'Heavens & Earths' within,

> . . . & when you enter into their Bosoms you walk
> In Heavens & Earths, as in your own Bosom you bear your
> Heaven,
> And Earth & all you behold; tho' it appears Without, it is
> Within,
> In your Imagination, of which the World of Mortality is but a
> shadow. (K709)

This is clear enough, and Berkeley had written as much. The things we perceive exist in being perceived, ultimately, according to Berkeley, by God; but for Blake 'God is Jesus' (K777) 'We are all co-existent with God – members of the Divine body. We are all partakers of the Divine nature'. (Crabb Robinson's *Diaries* p.225) What Blake calls the Last Judgement is the apokatastatic experience of this realization: 'Around the Throne Heaven is open'd & the Nature of Eternal Things Display'd, All Springing from the Divine Humanity. All beams from him'. (K612)

The concluding passage of *Jerusalem* describes, again, the flexibility of appearance – of time and space – in correspondence with 'states' of love and wisdom in the regenerated Man. 'The Four Senses are the Four Faces of Man & the Four Rivers of the Water of Life', (K773) and these are continually creating 'visionary forms dramatic'

> In new Expanses, creating exemplars of Memory & of Intellect,
> Creating Space, Creating Time, according to the wonders
> Divine
> Of Human Imagination . . .
> . . .
> . . . according to the Expansion or Contraction, the Translucence
> or Opakeness of Nervous fibres; such was the variation of
> Time & Space
> Which vary according as the Organs of Perception vary.
> (K746)

Thus Blake's last words in *Jerusalem* confirm his early affirmation in *The Marriage of Heaven and Hell* that 'If the doors of perception were cleansed everything would appear as it is, infinite' (K154), and 'the desire of Man being Infinite, the possession is Infinite & himself Infinite'. (K97)

Blake, Swedenborg and the Divine Human

THE POEM entitled 'The Divine Image' comes from *Songs of Innocence*, a collection of poems written for children and published in 1789, when Blake, was thirty-two years old. No-one, of whatever place, time, or religion, could fail to understand and to assent to the simple directness of its message:

> To Mercy, Pity, Peace and Love
> All pray in their distress;
> And to these virtues of delight
> Return their thankfulness.
>
> For Mercy, Pity, Peace, and Love
> Is God, our father dear,
> And Mercy, Pity, Peace, and Love,
> Is Man, his child and care.
>
> For Mercy has a human heart,
> Pity a human face,
> And Love, the human form divine,
> And Peace, the human dress.
>
> Then every man, of every clime,
> That prays in his distress,
> Prays to the human form divine,
> Love, Mercy, Pity, Peace.

And all must love the human form,
In heathen, turk or jew;
Where Mercy, Love, & Pity dwell
There God is dwelling too. (K117)

At first sight this might appear to be a simple statement of the Christian doctrine of the Incarnation, but there is much in the poem that might be unacceptable to the Apostolic Church, Catholic and Protestant alike; for Blake is not writing of the historical Jesus but of 'the human form in heathen, turk or jew' – a comprehensive phrase which embraces all the races and religions of mankind.

'The Divine Image' is the quintessence of Blake's prophetic message – that God is 'in the form of a man' and that the Incarnation is not particular but universal. Such is the power and certainty of Blake's genius that in simple words he cuts through all theological tangles to the mysterious heart of the Christian revelation. When Jesus affirmed 'I and the father are one' and 'he who has seen me has seen the father' his words were deemed blasphemous and led to his condemnation. Blake's religion, as he constantly declared, is 'the religion of Jesus' (by which he does not necessarily mean as taught by the Christian Church) and under the guise of 'poetic licence' the radical, not to say revolutionary content of his affirmation passes unnoticed. Such poems as 'The Divine Image' win the assent of the heart before their doctrinal implications become apparent. In Blake's terms Jesus, 'the true man', is the Imagination present in all. That innate Imagination assents to Blake's words. 'Knowledge is not by deduction, but Immediate by Perception or Sense at once. Christ addresses himself to the Man, not to his Reason.' (K774)

These words embody the spirit of a new age, a new apprehension of the Christian revelation. But when in *The Marriage of Heaven and Hell* Blake wrote that 'a new heaven is begun' he spoke not on his own authority but as a follower of Emanuel Swedenborg, of whose

London Society he was a member. Wonderful as are Blake's poems, his visionary paintings, his aphorisms, it is, in essence, the doctrines of Swedenborg that Blake's works embody and to which they lend poetry and eloquence. So, unawares, the teachings of Swedenborg have permeated the spiritual sensibility of the English nation, through Blake. Few of the ever-growing number who regard Blake as a prophet of the New Age are aware that the coherent and revolutionary interpretation of the Christian mysteries which underlies Blake's prophecies is that of Swedenborg; whose leading doctrines Blake summarized in *The Everlasting Gospel.*

The writings of Swedenborg, stilted and voluminous, written in Latin at a time when Latin was ceasing to be the common language of the learned, have none the less had a profound influence throughout Protestant Europe and beyond; Henry Corbin saw the seminal significance of Swedenborg, who he went so far as to describe as 'the Buddha of the West.' He was by profession neither philosopher nor theologian but a man of science. He spent much time in London where he had a strong following, and might even have been seen by Blake as a boy, for Swedenborg died in London in 1772, when Blake was fifteen. It seems likely that Blake's family were already Swedenborgians. Doubtless Swedenborg had predecessors in the millennial tradition, stemming from Joachim of Flora; but we must accept Swedenborg's word that his extraordinary prophetic insight came to him not by study but by what he described as an 'opening' of his consciousness which revealed to him the inner worlds which he calls the 'heavens' and the 'hells'; and which those who follow the terminology introduced by Henry Corbin would call the *mundus imaginalis*; worlds not in space, but in mankind's inner universe. In his visions it was shown to Swedenborg that a 'new church' had been established in the heavens, following a 'Last Judgement' passed on the Apostolic Church, which was to be superceded by the 'Church of the New Jerusalem', the last and perfect revelation of the nature of Jesus Christ as the

'Divine Humanity'; a mystery which had hitherto been imperfectly understood, but which was, in the New Church, to be fully revealed in the epiphany of the 'Divine Human'. This New Church, of which Swedenborg's writings are the scriptures, is to be the last in the six thousand years of the world's history from the creation to the end of days and the coming of the Kingdom. There have already been, according to Swedenborg, twenty-six such churches, from the time of Adam, through a succession of prophetic revelations made to the Patriarchs, to Noah, Abraham, Moses, Solomon, and within the Christian era the churches of Paul, Constantine, Charlemagne and Luther; each of these representing some new realization—or revelation—which is to reach its term and perfect fulfilment in a total affirmation of the humanity of God and the divinity of man, their unity and identity. In his setting-out of the Leading Doctrines of the Church of the New Jerusalem Swedenborg declares that: 'The Lord is God from eternity' and the Divine Human is not merely the Son of God but God himself. 'God and man, in the Lord . . . are not two, but one person, yet, altogether one . . . He is the God of heaven and earth'. The Divine Humanity is almighty; or, as Blake simply says, 'God is Jesus.' (K777) Since in this teaching the oneness of the human and the divine is total, it follows that the Christian revelation can go no farther, man and God being one, not only in the historic person of Jesus Christ but for the Christ within the whole human race.

Jung has written in criticism of the Christian Church that, if not in principle, at all events in practice, the divine Being has been envisaged as outside man and the Redemption (in the doctine of the Atonement) also as an occurrence outside man, occurring once only, in history. It is true that the Mass is held to be not a commemoration of that event, but a timeless re-enactment; but even so, that Mystery, as commonly taught and understood, is an external and historical event. Jesus Christ, moreover, is an exceptional being, virtually a demi-god in the Pagan sense, not fully human. Jung in his remarkable work, *Answer to Job*—admired by

Henry Corbin* – and expressing the mature thought of a lifetime on the meaning of Christianity, writes that

> Christ by his descent, conception and birth, is a half-god in the classical sense. He is virginally begotten by the Holy Ghost and, as he is not a creaturely human being, has no inclination to sin. The infection of evil was in his case precluded by the preparations for the Incarnation. He therefore stands more on the divine than on the human level. (*Answer to Job* p.669)

The same is true of the Virgin Mary: 'As a consequence of her immaculate conception Mary is already different from other mortals, and this fact is confirmed by her assumption.' (ibid. Note.) Thus salvation is available to humankind through the external intervention of these superhuman personages. In making this criticism of Christianity Jung makes no mention of Swedenborg, whose teachings did in fact raise and respond to many of his own criticisms, in calling for an interiorization of the Christian mysteries of the Incarnation, Passion and Resurrection. This is the more strange because Jung is known to have read Swedenborg's works early in life. Swedenborg gives an actual date – 1757 (which was, incidentally, the date of Blake's birth) – when a 'Last Judgement' had been passed on the Apostolic Church 'in the heavens' – that is to say in mankind's inner worlds – to be followed by an epiphany of the Divine Humanity in His full glory in the inner worlds or 'heavens'. With this inner event a new kind of realization, a new kind of consciousness, began to dawn within Christendom, following the interiorization of the Apostolic teaching. This Last Judgment was not an outer event, in time and in history, but an inner event, which would, not dramatically, but gradually, make itself apparent also in the outer world of history. A new church is thus a

* See his review 'La Sophia Eternelle' in *La Revue de Culture Européen*, No.5 (1953).

new consciousness. Without invoking the idea of 'evolution' (as understood by materialist science) we are to understand Swedenborg's concept of the twenty-seven churches as a progressive revelation in time and history. This is entirely in keeping with the linear view of time common to all the Abrahamic religions (Judaism, Christianity and Islam) and indeed without such a conception time and history become meaningless. Blake indeed saw the twenty-seven churches rather as cyclic than linear, a progressive darkening of the paradisal vision from Adam to Jesus Christ, followed by a progressive recovery to be fulfilled in the 'second coming' in the inner worlds. This event completes the cycle which leads humankind back to the Paradisal state from which we have fallen.

What is under consideration is an event whose nature is rather a subtle change of awareness than a temporal fact. It seems that such a change in the understanding of the nature of spiritual events did begin to manifest itself at that time, which has continued to grow like a plant from a small seed. Swedenborg's seed fell on fertile ground in the spirit of William Blake; and our presence here at the University of St. John of Jerusalem, dedicated to an understanding of the Imaginal, the inner universe, is an expression—one amongst others—of this new understanding, in a world where the old foundations seem inadequate. It may well be that in the future our own time will be seen not as the age of the triumph of materialist science but as the breakdown of that phase and the beginning of just such an 'opening' of humanity's inner worlds as Swedenborg prophetically experienced and foresaw.

This theme is a central one for Jung, who in his *Answer to Job* sets forth at length a view of the Bible in which, from Job to the Incarnation of Jesus Christ, there is what he calls 'a tendency for God to become man'. This tendency is already implicit in Genesis, when by a special act of creation Jahweh created man, the image of God. Jung is, of course, using the terms not of theology but of psychology and is therefore writing of changes in human consciousness of the Divine Being, and not of changes in God himself in an absolute sense. Jung writes:

> 'In omniscience, there had existed from all eternity a knowledge of the human nature of God or of the divine nature of man. That is why, long before Genesis was written, we find corresponding testimonies in ancient Egyptian records. Preparations, however, are not in themselves creative events, but only stages in the process of becoming conscious. It was only quite late that we realized (or rather, are beginning to realize) that God is Reality itself and therefore – last but not least – man. This realization is a millennial process. (para. 631)

Jung sees this process foreshadowed in the story of Job – the type of the human encounter with the divine. The God of the Book of Job is so totally other that Job seems to himself to be insignificant, powerless, without recourse – except to God himself; and Jung is in agreement with theologians who have seen in Job's words 'I know that my redeemer liveth, and that he shall stand in the latter day upon the earth . . . yet in my flesh shall I see God' a foreshadowing of the Incarnation:

> The life of Christ is just what it had to be if it is the life of a god and a man at the same time. It is a *symbolus*, a bringing together of heterogeneous natures, rather as if Job and Yahweh were combined in a single personality. Yahweh's intention to become man, which resulted from his collision with Job, is fulfilled in Christ's life and suffering. (p.409)

On the way to this realization, Jung points out, we have Ezekiel's vision of the 'Son of Man', which reappears in the Book of Daniel, and later (about 100 B.C.) in the Book of Enoch. Ezekiel is himself addressed as 'Son of Man' – the man on the throne whom he beheld in his vision; and hence a prefiguration of the much later revelation in Christ. Daniel had a vision of the 'Ancient of Days', to whom 'with the clouds of heaven there came one like the son of man'. Here the 'son of man' is no longer the prophet himself but a son of the 'Ancient of Days' in his own right.

The power of Swedenborg's revelation, and of Blake's prophetic writings lies in the reality of what they describe, a growing inner awareness on which we cannot go back. Jung, and even Freud, were aware of this process of interiorization of the Mysteries, but they were not the first to challenge the externalized consciousness of post-Cartesian science; 'the Divine is not in Space' Swedenborg affirmed, 'although the Divine is omnipresent with every man in the world, and with every angel in heaven.' (*Divine Love and Wisdom* 7) This, it may be said, has always been so and is implicit in every religious tradition; yet as a fact of the history of two thousand years of Christendom, the realization has been progressive and come but slowly.

Swedenborg strove to remove the identification of reality with an external material order. Space is a function of the natural body but the human spirit is capable of the omnipresence of the non-spatial. Furthermore, it is not God who is omnipresent spirit while man exists in space, because 'God is Very Man' the human universe is likewise boundless spirit, as God is. He writes:

> In all the heavens there is no other idea of God than the idea of a man; the reason is, that heaven as a whole, and in every part, is in form as a man and the Divine, which is with the angels, constitutes heaven; and thought proceeds according to the form of heaven; wherefore it is impossible for the angels to think of God otherwise. Hence it is that all those in the world who are conjoined with heaven [that is with the inner worlds] when they think interiorly in themselves, that is, in their spirit, think of God in a like manner. For this cause that God is a Man. The form of heaven affects this, which in its greatest and in its least things is like itself. (DLW 11)

Heaven in its whole and in every part is 'in form as a man'; and because man was created 'after the image and likeness of God', 'the ancients, from the wise to the simple'—from Abraham to the primitive Africans—thought of God as a man. This is not anthropomorphism in the sense in which the word is currently understood, as a projection of the human image upon the divine mystery, but rather the reverse, a recognition of the divine image imprinted on the inner nature of humankind, as 'the Divine Human', to use Swedenborg's term. 'All is Human, Mighty, Divine', Blake writes; and summarises the Swedenborgian teaching in a quatrain:

> God Appears & God is Light
> To those poor Souls who dwell in Night,
> But does a Human Form Display
> To those who dwell in Realms of day. (K434)

These lines are the reversal of the 'enlightened' view that we cease to see God in human form as we learn more about 'the universe' as natural fact. The ultimate knowledge, according to Blake and Swedenborg, is that the universe is contained in the Divine Humanity.

> All Things are comprehended in their Eternal Forms in the divine body of the Saviour, the True Vine of Eternity, The Human Imagination. (K605–6)

Thus we are given a conception of man totally other than that of a materialist science: Man in his spiritual being is boundless and contains not a part of his universe but its wholeness and infinitude. The 'body' of the Divine Human is not contained in natural space but contains all things in itself. Swedenborg writes:

> His human body cannot be thought of as great or small, or of any stature, because this also attributes space; and hence He is the same in the first things as the last and in the greatest things and the least; and moreover the Human is the inner-

> most of every created thing, but apart from space. (DLW285)

Swedenborg uses a strange but cogent argument for the humanity of the Divine: that the attributes of God would be inconceivable except in human terms; and since God is knowable only in human terms He must therefore possess human attributes:

> that God could not have created the universe and all things thereof, unless He were a Man, may be very clearly comprehended by an intelligent person from this ground that . . . in God there is love and wisdom, there is mercy and clemency, and also that there is absolute Goodness and Truth, because these things are from Him. And because he cannot deny these things, neither can he deny that God is a Man: for not one of these things is possible abstracted from man: man is their subject, and to separate them from their subject is to say that they are not. Think of wisdom and place it outside man. Is there anything? . . . It must be wisdom in a form such as man has, it must be in all his form, not one thing can be wanting for wisdom to be in it. In a word, the form of wisdom is a man; and because man is the form of wisdom, he is also the form of love, mercy, clemency, good, and truth, because these make one with wisdom. (DLW286)

It is for these reasons, Swedenborg argues, that Man is said to be created in the image of God, because into the form of love and wisdom. It cannot be that man invented God in his own image, since that image is already imprinted in us in our very being. The argument is a subtle one; and although it could be asked, could not God have created beings and universes other than man, the same argument would in every case apply: whatever their attributes these too would bear the image and imprint of their creator and source. Blake, who had read and annotated Swedenborg's *Divine Love and Wisdom* with evident delight might, when he addressed 'The

Divine Image' Mercy, Pity, Peace and Love have been thinking of this very passage.

Swedenborg dismisses the idea of those who think of God as other than as a Man, and 'of the divine attributes otherwise than as God as a man; because separated from man they are figments of the mind. God is very Man, from whom every Man is a man according to his reception of love and wisdom'. (DLW289)

So it is that

> Mercy has the human heart
> Pity the human face
> And love the human form divine
> And peace the human dress.

'The human form divine' is not the natural body idolatrously glorified but the spiritual form of our human nature.

In understanding that when he wrote these words, so luminously simple, Blake is propounding Swedenborgian doctrine, it becomes perfectly clear that no humanism is implicit in his assigning the human attributes to God, the source and author of our humanity. Swedenborg wrote that 'in all forms and uses there is a certain image of man.' and that 'all uses from primes to ultimates, from ultimates to primes, have relation to all things of man and correspondences with him, and therefore man in a certain image is a universe; and conversely the universe viewed as to its uses is man in an image'. (DLW317) Swedenborg draws the conclusion that it is for this reason that man is called a microcosm; since the universe is totally present in all its parts. Or again, in Blake's words, 'One thought fills immensity'. What Swedenborg is saying in his stilted style, and Blake is repeating in what to his contemporaries seemed 'wild' poetic ravings, is in fact of extreme subtlety and great profundity—that human consciousness contains its universe. This is a return to the ancient teaching, as found for example in the *Hermetica*, that mind is not in space but all spaces and whatever these contain, in mind. To have reaffirmed this realization in eighteenth-century England attests to an insight so extraordinary that it can only be described—and Swedenborg did so describe it—as a prophetic revelation.

Swedenborg affirms continually that the universal heaven is in the form of a man, and 'each society in heaven, be it large or small, is so likewise; hence also an angel is a man, for an angel is heaven in its least form'. Thus every part down to the smallest 'heaven in its least form' is infinite, and the Divine Human an infinite whole made up of infinite wholes, and 'the universal heaven consists of myriads of myriads of angels.' (Here it must be said that Swedenborg's angels are also men, but discarnate. The word angel, as he uses it, is not to be understood in the sense of the Near-Eastern religions, or indeed of the Christian Fathers, or Dionysius the Areopagite's *Celestial Hierarchies*.)

The human form is present throughout the universe alike in its greatest and in its least parts. Swedenborg writes that

> In God Man infinite things are distinctly one. It is well known that God is Infinite, for he is called the Infinite. He is not infinite by this alone, that He is very Esse and Existere in Himself, but because there are Infinite things in Him. (DLW17)

The 'vision of light' Blake described in a letter to a friend is purely Swedenborgian; every infinitesimal part of nature is human—and this is his answer to Newton's theory that light is made of 'particles':

> In particles bright
> The jewels of Light
> Distinct shone & clear.
> Amaz'd & in fear
> I each particle gazed,
> Astonish'd, Amazed;

For each was a Man
Human-form'd. Swift I ran,
For they beckon'd to me
Remote by the Sea,
Saying: Each grain of Sand,
Every Stone on the Land,
Each rock & each hill,
Each fountain & rill,
Each herb & each tree,
Mountain, hill, earth & sea,
Cloud, Meteor & Star,
Are Men Seen Afar. (K804–5)

Swedenborg's Grand Man of the heavens is a concept of great splendour. In this Divine Man or Human Divine all lives are contained, individually and as angelic societies within the one life of the Divine Humanity; and so down to every inhabitant of heaven who is 'every one in his own heaven' and the whole is reflected in each. 'The Lord leads all in the universal heaven as if they were one angel' and in the same way 'an angelic society sometimes appears as one man in the form of an angel. (*Heaven and Hell* 51) So 'when the Lord himself appears in the midst of the angels, he does not appear encompassed by a multitude but as one in an angelic form.' 'I have seen', he writes of a visionary society, that 'when at a distance it appears as one, and on its approach, as a multitude.' And again it is hard to know whether Blake is describing his own vision or paraphrasing Swedenborg when he writes: 'these various States I have seen in my imagination; when distant they appear as One Man but as you approach they appear multitudes of nations.' (K607) Blake summarizes the essence of the Swedenborgian vision of the Grand Man in a passage several times repeated in the Prophetic Books:

Then those in Great Eternity met in the Council of God
As one Man, for contracting their Exalted Senses

> They behold Multitude, or Expanding they behold as one,
> As One Man all the Universal Family; & that One Man
> They call Jesus the Christ, & they in him & he in them
> Live in Perfect harmony, in Eden the land of life,
> Consulting As One Man above the Mountain of Snowdon
> Sublime. (K277)

Eden the land of life is the *mundus imaginalis*, the 'bosom of God', our native place and state.

In affirming the humanity of God Swedenborg is nevertheless remote from what is now called 'humanism'; for man is (in Blake's words) only 'a form and organ of life' and the life of every individual, of every community, of the whole creation, is 'from the Lord'. No man's life belongs to himself, each is a recipient of the one life. Thus, whereas Blake wrote that 'God is Man & exists in us & we in him', (K775) this is no more or less than the teaching of St. John's Gospel and the words of Jesus, 'as thou, Father, art in me, and I in thee, that they also may be one in us'. Created beings and men exist by virtue of what Swedenborg calls the 'influx' of the one divine life. This influx is through the inner worlds; the outer world of natural appearances is the mirror of spiritual realities, but has itself no substance. (This is of course the teaching of Plotinus on Nature, and of other Platonic writers). But the outer form—whether of human being or animal, plant or mineral—is the 'correspondence' of their living nature.

In *Divine Love and Wisdom* Swedenborg writes:

> . . . the spiritual world in external appearance is quite similar to the natural world. Lands appear there, mountains, hills, valleys, planes, fields, lakes, rivers, springs of water, as in the natural world . . . Paradises also appear there, gardens, groves, woods, and in them trees and shrubs of all kinds bearing fruit and seeds; also plants, flowers, herbs and

> grasses . . . Animals appear there, birds and fish of every kind. (DLW32)

In his systematic manner Swedenborg spells out the presence in the 'heavens', of the mineral, vegetable and animal kingdoms. In Swedenborg's 'heavens', Blake's Imagination, whom both call the Divine Human, the whole universe is contained in its infinite variety as the diversification of the single being of the Divine Humanity. The realities mirrored in nature belong to the Imaginal world – in Blake's terms the Imagination. Blake too insists that the Imaginal world is a plenitude of forms:

> Many suppose that before the Creation All was Solitude & Chaos. This is the most pernicious Idea that can enter the Mind, as it . . . Limits All Existence to Creation & to Chaos, to the Time & Space fixed by the Corporeal Vegetative Eye . . . Externity Exists & All things in Eternity, Independent of Creation (K614)

In an early work, *Vala, or The Four Zoas* Blake describes the whole natural creation striving – 'groaning and travailing', in the words of St. Paul – to bring forth the human:

> Man looks out in tree & herb & fish & bird & beast
> Collecting up the scatter'd portions of his immortal body
> Into the Elemental forms of every thing that grows.
> . . .
> In pain he sighs, in pain he labours in his universe,
> Screaming in birds over the deep, & howling in the wolf
> Over the slain, & moaning in the cattle & in the winds
> . . .
> And in the cries of birth & in the groans of death his voice
> Is heard throughout the Universe: wherever a grass grows
> Or a leaf buds, The Eternal Man is seen, is heard, is felt
> And all his sorrows, till he reassumes his ancient bliss.
> (K355–6)

Humanity, the immortal body 'distributed' as the Platonists would say, in the 'many' must be reassumed into the 'one', the bosom of God, the Human Imagination. In that universe microcosm and macrocosm are one.

I mentioned earlier C.G. Jung's highly significant criticisms of the Christian Church for its conversion of the figures of Jesus Christ, and in the Catholic Church the Virgin Mary likewise, into what have been to all intents and purposes pagan demigods. Jung's criticisms of Christianity have indeed been cogent, and he has played a significant part in calling for an interiorization of the Christian Mysteries. In the Introduction to his *Psychology and Alchemy* he writes:

> We can accuse Christianity of arrested development if we are determined to excuse our own shortcomings. In speaking therefore not of the deepest and best understanding of Christianity but of the superficialities and disastrous misunderstandings that are plain to see. The demand made by the *imitatio Christi* – that we should follow the ideal and seek to become like it – ought logically to have the result of developing and exalting the inner man. In actual fact, however, the ideal has been turned into an external object of worship, and it is precisely this veneration for the object that prevents it from reaching down into the depths of the soul and transforming it into a wholeness in keeping with the ideal. Accordingly the divine mediator stands outside as an image, while man remains fragmentary and untouched in the deepest of him. (para. 7)

– and later in the same work

> It may easily happen, therefore, that a Christian who believes in all the sacred figures is still undeveloped and unchanged in his innermost soul because he has 'all God outside' and does

> not experience him in the soul. . . . Yes, everything is to be found outside – in image and in word, in Church and Bible – but never inside . . . Too few people have experienced the divine image as the innermost possession of their own souls. Christ only meets them from without, never within the soul. (para. 12)

This summons to our time to discover the God within may be seen as perhaps Jung's greatest contribution – and a very great one it is. Jung makes no mention of Swedenborg as a predecessor and prophet of just such a transformation of consciousness as he himself wished to see. Swedenborg, on his part, would have seen Jung as one fulfilment of his prophecy, his vision of a Last Judgment in the heavens passed on the Apostolic Church, to be followed by the appearance of the Lord in the inner heavens. Jung writes of the 'God-image', the divine signature or archetype, imprinted in every soul. Accused by theologians of 'psychologism' for making his appeal to his God-image and thereby of 'deifying the soul', Jung replies, 'when I say as a psychologist that God is an archetype, I mean by that the "type" in the psyche. The word "type" is, as we know, derived from τυπος to "strike" or "imprint"; thus an archetype pre-supposes an imprinter.' (para. 15) The argument is very close to that of Swedenborg, that human qualities must mirror divine qualities. In this respect Henry Corbin, in reviewing Jung's *Answer to Job*, defends Jung, himself being deeply concerned with defining and discovering the 'imaginal' world.

> True, C.G. Jung chooses not to speak otherwise than as a psychologist, and deals only with psychology; he does not claim to be a theologian or even a philosopher of religion. But having said 'Only a psychologist, only psychology' one has the sudden sense of having committed a grave injustice, of associating oneself by that way of speaking with all those who, mistrusting for one reason or another the implications of Jung's works, close the matter after each one with the

> comment 'it is *nothing but* psychology'. But one may well ask oneself what they have done with their *soul*, with their *Psyche* to dismiss it in this way and to dare to speak of it in terms of being 'nothing but that'. So why when one has shown that there are psychological factors which correspond to divine figures, do some people find it necessary to cry blasphemy as if all were lost and those figures devaluated?

Swedenborg too had insisted that the imprint of the infinite and eternal is within every form; and moreover that the infinite and eternal is present in the infinite variety of things, 'in that no substance state or thing in the created universe can ever be the same or identical with any other'. So that in none of the things that fill the universe can any sameness be produced to all eternity. This (he continues) is 'perspicuously evident in the variety of faces of all human beings; not one face exists in the whole world which is the same as another, neither can exist in all eternity'. (DLW315) Here Swedenborg is using the word imprint in exactly Jung's sense. Yet by influx all these are forms of the divine image, in Blake's words

> . . . the Divine
> Humanity who is the Only General and Universal Form
> To which all Lineaments tend & seek with love & sympathy.
> (K672)

There is not one image or face of God but an infinity of images, an infinity of faces. The implications are overwhelming for it follows that every human face in the world is, insofar as it is open to the divine influx, one of the myriad faces of God.

Swedenborg claimed for his Church of the New Jerusalem that it is to be the ultimate Christian Revelation and understanding of the Son of God in his Divine Humanity; and indeed it is not possible to conceive a closer union of God and Man than in this universal influx of divinity in all creation and in all humankind.

To turn once again to Jung's remarkable diagnosis of our present situation, *Answer to Job*. He describes the gradual emergence, in the Bible, of the idea of God as Man, becoming ever clearer from Job to Ezekiel to Daniel, to the Book of Enoch, and finally to the Incarnation of Jesus Christ. But Jung, like Swedenborg, does not see the gradual realization as ending there. As Swedenborg in the symbol of his twenty-seven Churches sees, from the time of Jesus, not one but several successive churches emerging and falling into decay, so does Jung see the Christian Revelation as incomplete. As a psychologist he had witnessed, over a long lifetime, the pressure within the human soul itself towards some further understanding. Just as Swedenborg saw the awaited completion as a perfected understanding of the nature of Jesus Christ as omnipresent in all, Jung saw it as an awaited incarnation within poor imperfect earthly humankind; which indeed was what Swedenborg himself understood by his New Church but saw it as already accomplished. Jung points out that Jesus himself in sending to his disciples 'the spirit of truth', the Holy Ghost, envisages a continuing realization of God in his children, which amounts to a continuance of the Incarnation. He reminds his disciples that he had told them that they were 'gods'. The believers or chosen ones are children of God, all 'fellow-heirs with Christ'. Of this teaching the Fourth Gospel is full;

> the indwelling of the Holy Ghost means nothing less than an approximation of the believer to the status of God's son. One can therefore understand what is meant by the remark 'you are gods'. The deifying effect of the Holy Ghost is naturally assisted by the *imago Dei* stamped on the elect. God, in the shape of the Holy Ghost, puts up his tent in man, for he is obviously minded to realize himself continually not only in Adam's descendants, but in an indefinitely large number of believers, and possibly in mankind as a whole.' (para. 656)

Only in suffering the limitations of the 'empirical human being', Jung insists, can God truly suffer the human condition, for in a

Christ exempt from sin he could not do so. Jung points out that throughout the history of the Church, both Catholic and Protestant, whereas the worship of the Son has been practised and encouraged, the presence of the Holy Spirit within the soul has been played down, to say the least. Jung cites the instance of the banning of the writings of Eckhart on account of certain passages in which this teaching is made too clear for the liking of the apostolic hierarchy. Again Corbin supports Jung, commenting that

> The action of the Paraclete, metaphysically so important, is wholly undesirable for the good organization of a Church, for it eludes all control. In consequence there was to be energetic affirmation of the uniqueness of the event of the Incarnation, and the progressive indwelling of the Holy Spirit in man either discouraged or ignored. Whoever felt himself to be inspired by the Holy Spirit to 'deviations' was a heretic, his extirpation and extermination both necessary and in accordance with Satan's liking.

This is the Protestant point of view, shared by Jung, son of a Lutheran Pastor, by Henry Corbin, by Swedenborg and by William Blake. It is at the heart of the great and unresolved division within Christendom.

The Millennial prophesies of Joachim of Flora have echoed throughout subsequent history his foretelling of a third phase of Christendom which he called the Age of the Holy Spirit, which was to follow the ages of the Father and of the Son. Within this tradition Swedenborg and Blake are situated, and indeed Jung himself. Jung writes on the sending of the Paraclete:

> Since he is the Third Person of the Deity, this is as much as to say that *God will be begotten in creaturely man.* This implies a tremendous change in man's status, for he is now raised to sonship, and almost to the position of a man-god. With this the prefiguration in Ezekiel and Enoch, where, as we saw, the

> title of 'Son of Man' was already conferred on the creaturely man, is fulfilled. But that puts man, despite his continuing sinfulness, in the position of the mediator, the unifier of God and creature. Christ probably had this incalculable possibility in mind when he said, '. . . he who believes in me, will also do the works that I do; and greater works than these will he do', and referring to the sixth verse of the Eighty-second Psalm, 'I say, "You are gods, sons of the Most High, all of you" he added, "and scripture cannot be broken".' (para. 692)

I have quoted Jung at length because his understanding of Christianity as a progressive revelation stands within the mystical mainstream represented by Joachim of Flora, Eckhardt, Swedenborg and Blake.

In some respects Swedenborg's Christianity lies within the mainstream of orthodoxy. Blake indeed reproached Swedenborg because he had not in fact taught anything new. In *The Marriage of Heaven and Hell* Blake writes: 'Now hear a plain fact: Swedenborg has not written one new truth. Now hear another: he has written all the old falsehoods.' (K157) What Blake chiefly held against Swedenborg was that he lays excessive stress on moral virtue, placing the virtuous in the heavens and the evil-doers in the hells. Blake himself saw in Divine Humanity as embracing the wholeness of life, both heaven and hell, reason and energy, the darkness and the light in a holiness and a wholeness beyond what humankind calls good and evil in terms of the moral laws of this world. Like Jung, Blake understood that there can be no completeness if any part of the totality of the Divine Human is excluded. It is probable that Blake did not, either, share Swedenborg's view of the unique and exceptional nature of the historical Jesus Christ. He does profess 'the religion of Jesus' but by this he certainly did not mean Apostolic Christianity but the religion that Jesus himself practised. Blake's view is that 'Jesus, the Imagination', the Divine Human, is born, lives and dies in every life. God is born in every birth, not in one only; when Jehovah

> . . . stood in the gates of the Victim, & he appeared
> A weeping Infant in the gates of Birth in the midst of Heaven.

– he is born not in one but in all:

> . . . a little weeping Infant pale reflected
> Multitudinous in the Looking Glass of Enitharmon.
> (K697)

– that is, in the 'mirror' of the natural world. The one Babe of the eternal Incarnation is reflected not in one but in multitudes of births, in every birth. For Blake's Divine Humanity says,

> In Me all Eternity
> Must pass thro' condemnation and awake beyond the Grave.
> (K662)

Man is not once but continually redeemed in 'the Body of Jesus' – that is, in the Divine Humanity in whom all participate; and the 'Divine Similitude' – the face of God – is seen

> In loves and tears of brothers, sisters, sons, fathers and friends,
> Which if Man ceases to behold, he ceases to exist. (K664)

The 'Divine Family' is 'as one Man'

> . . . and they were One in Him. A Human Vision!
> Human Divine, Jesus the Saviour, blessed for ever and ever.
> (K667)

Thus the 'Divine Humanity' is not a single individual but a family; and Blake goes so far as to condemn explicitly the teaching that the Lord, or any of the 'eternal states' which constitute the human universe is or ever could be represented by any single individual. In this Blake certainly goes beyond Swedenborg, at least in relation to the Jesus Christ of history. How strongly Blake held this view is clear from these lines from *Jerusalem*:

Los cries: 'No Individual ought to appropriate to Himself
Or to his Emanation [that is, his feminine counterpart] any of the
 Universal Characteristics
Of David or of Eve, of the Woman or of the Lord,
Of Reuben or of Benjamin, of Joseph or Judah or Levi.
Those who dare appropriate to themselves Universal Attributes
Are the Blasphemous Selfhoods, & must be broken asunder.
A Vegetated Christ & a Virgin Eve are the Hermaphroditic
Blasphemy; by his Maternal Birth he is that Evil-One
And his Maternal Humanity must be put off Eternally,
Lest the Sexual Generation swallow up Regeneration.'

(K736–7)

—and the passage ends with the invocation, 'Come Lord Jesus, take on thee the Satanic Body of Holiness!' The Divine Humanity is invoked to put on a generated body in order to transcend his natural humanity, transmitted by the mother. To Blake mortal generation is binding of an immortal spirit into the cruel bondage of mortality:

Thou, Mother of my Mortal part,
With cruelty didst mould my Heart,
And with false self-deceiving tears
Didst bind my Nostrils, Eyes, & Ears:

Didst close my Tongue in senseless clay,
And me to Mortal Life betray.
The Death of Jesus set me free:
Then what have I to do with thee? (K220)

This poem from *Songs of Experience* is far indeed from those Christmas lullabies of the Nativity to which we are accustomed, but it is a concise summary of Swedenborg's teaching. Readers unfamiliar with Swedenborg's view of the place of the Mother in the Mystery of the Incarnation must find Blake's treatment of the Incarnation in this and other passages extremely puzzling. But the Leading Doctrines of the Church of the New Jerusalem, far from supporting the view of the Immaculate Conception of the Virgin Mary, see the Mother as the means through which Jesus Christ took on sin. Both Swedenborg and Blake had confronted the question which was later to present itself to Jung, of how the not-quite-human son of a mother herself born without sin could experience the human condition. If, as Swedenborg taught, Jesus came to 'glorify his human' by overcoming the successive temptations 'admitted into his human from the mother' in order to 'put on a human from the Divine within him, which is the Divine Human, and the Son of God' (*Four Leading Doctrines of the New Church*, 4 & 64) then the mother is indeed, as in Blake's poem, 'cruel' and the source of evil not of good. Swedenborg is quite categorical in his insistence that the natural humanity inherited by Jesus Christ from his earthly mother

> cannot be transmuted into the Divine Essence nor, can it be commixed with it . . . thus it follows that the Lord put off the human from the mother which, in itself, was like the human of another man, and thus material, and put on the human from the Father, which, in itself, was like His Divine, and thus substantial; and from which the Human also was made divine'. (77–8)

—not, be it understood, by the elevation of what Blake calls 'a Vegetated Christ' but, on the contrary, by putting off his natural humanity. Blake summarizes the Swedenborgian teaching. In *The Everlasting Gospel*, which is a summary of Swedenborg's *Leading Doctrines of the New Church*, Blake spells out this teaching:

> Was Jesus Born of a Virgin Pure
> With narrow Soul & looks demure?

> If he intended to take on Sin
> The Mother should an Harlot been,
> Just such a one as Magdalen
> With seven devils in her Pen. (K756)

This teaching Blake summarised in the two lines,

> He took on Sin in the Virgin's Womb,
> And put it off on the Cross & Tomb. (K749)

and he concludes this passage with the line: 'To be worship'd by the Church of Rome'. He is in this sense right that the Roman Church specifically teaches the resurrection of the physical body and that the natural man ascends to heaven.

Thus in his doctrine that 'The Lord put off the human from the Mother, and put on the Human from the Divine in himself which is called the father' Swedenborg anticipated and resolved Jung's later question as to the incompleteness of the Incarnation. What Jung saw as a future possibility Swedenborg and Blake saw as already accomplished in the Mystery of the Incarnation, which had not hitherto been properly understood. The lines just quoted are taken from a late poem by Blake entitled *The Everlasting Gospel*, a series of fragments which are in fact all expositions of Swedenborg's Leading Doctrines. One fragment expands at length the necessity that the Mother of Jesus should be a vehicle of sins and not 'a Virgin pure/With narrow Soul & looks demure'. He comes very close indeed to Jung when he writes

> Or what was it, which he took on
> That he might bring Salvation?
> A Body subject to be Tempted
> From neither pain or grief Exempted?
> Or such a body as might not feel
> The passions that with Sinners deal? (K756)

Yet in affirming the indwelling of the Divine Human in mankind, and the total humanity of Jesus in taking on a fully human, fully sinful inheritance, how far are Swedenborg, Blake, Jung from any humanistic intent of exalting the natural humanity—the mortal selfhood—to a god-like status, usurping the name of humanity from the divine principle in man and affirming the supremacy of the natural man. Swedenborg insists that it is only through putting off his natural humanity through temptations overcome, and finally on the Cross, that Jesus glorified the Divine Humanity of the Father. Blake, who saw the divine image in every human face, wrote:

> The Spirit of Jesus is continual forgiveness of Sin: he who waits to be righteous before he enters into the Saviour's kingdom, the Divine Body, will never enter there. I am perhaps the most sinful of men. I pretend not to holiness: yet I pretend to love, to see, to converse with daily as man with man, & the more to have an interest in the Friend of Sinners. (K621)

And finally Jung, who has most powerfully carried into our own day the mystery of the divine presence in every man: Jung concludes his *Answer to Job* with these words, on the paradox of the divine presence that indwells 'the ordinary mortal who is not free from original sin':

> even the enlightened person remains what he is, and is never more than his limited ego before the One who dwells within him, whose form has no knowable boundaries, who encompasses him on all sides, fathomless as the abyss of the earth and vast as the sky. (para. 758)

The City in Blake's Prophetic Poetry

Blake is of all English poets the supreme poet of the City, and what he wrote on his own city, London, must surely have meaning for any city; for what he had – has – to say about London has little to do with such matters as a town-planner, or a writer on buildings of architectural interest might have to tell us. For Blake a city is a living organism, 'a Human awful wonder of God', as he wrote; it is the inner lives of the inhabitants as these act and interact upon one another. Of this invisible city, composed of a multitude of lives, the city of stone and brick, of streets and buildings, of palaces and churches, is only the image and expression. For Blake, a Londoner born, his city is above all human:

> I behold London, a Human awful wonder of God!
> He says: 'Return, Albion, return! I give myself for thee.
> My Streets are my Ideas of Imagination.
> Awake Albion, awake! and let us awake up together.
> My Houses are Thoughts: my Inhabitants, Affections,
> The children of my thoughts walking within my blood-vessels.'
> (K665)

Throughout his life Blake continued to listen to the unspoken thoughts of his city's collective life and to that of 'the Giant Albion', the collective life of the English nation:

So spoke London, immortal Guardian! I heard in Lambeth's
shades.
In Felpham I heard and saw the Visions of Albion.
I write in South Molton Street what I both see and hear
In regions of Humanity, in London's opening streets. (K665)

Blake had lived in Lambeth during the early years of his marriage; in Felpham on the Sussex coast for three years, then back in London, in South Molton Street, in the very heart of the city which he never again left. Every city has its collective identity, its special human character:

Verulam! Canterbury! venerable parent of men,
Generous immortal Guardian, golden clad! for Cities
Are Men, fathers of multitudes, and Rivers and Mountains
Are also men! every thing is Human, mighty!
sublime! (K665)

—and he names other cities, 'Edinburgh, cloth'd with fortitude', York, Selsea, Chichester, Oxford, Bath, Durham, Lincoln, Carlisle, Ely, Norwich, Peterborough—all the principle cities of England, and each with its own character.

Bath, mild Physician of Eternity, mysterious power
Whose springs are unsearchable and knowledge infinite:
Hereford, ancient Guardian of Wales, whose hands
Builded the mountain palaces of Eden, stupendous works!
Lincoln, Durham & Carlisle, Counsellors of Los,
And Ely, Scribe of Los, whose pen no other hand
Dare touch: Oxford, immortal Bard, with eloquence
Divine he wept over Albion speaking the words of God
In mild perswasion, bringing leaves of the Tree of Life.
(K676)

A certain amount of historical research already has, or without great difficulty could, be done in order to explicate such obscure statements as

> Go thou to Skofield: ask him if he is Bath, or if he is Canterbury.
> Tell him to be no more dubious (K640)

It has been suggested that when Blake writes of 'the healing leaves of Oxford' he might even have had Shelley in mind, although indeed many other 'healing leaves' have been penned in that city, to which Blake could have referred.

In the poem *London* there is no description of the appearance of the city, whose essence is evoked in human terms:

> I wander thro' each charter'd street
> Near where the charter'd Thames does flow,
> And mark in every face I meet
> Marks of weakness, marks of woe.
>
> In every cry of every Man,
> In every Infant's cry of fear,
> In every voice, in every ban,
> The mind-forg'd manacles I hear.
>
> How the Chimney-sweeper's cry
> Every black'ning Church appals;
> And the hapless Soldier's sigh
> Runs in blood down Palace walls.
>
> But most thro' midnight streets I hear
> How the youthful Harlot's curse
> Blasts the newborn Infant's tear
> And blights with plagues the Marriage hearse. (K216)

Yet Blake's London was not wholly, as for that later poet of London, T. S. Eliot (himself much indebted to Blake for his spiritual topography) a waste land, a scene in hell: rather its life spanned the whole range of human joy and sorrow. London, in

Songs of Experience, is depicted as an old man led by a little child; and Blake used the same depiction years later, in *Jerusalem*, to illustrate the words

> I see London, blind and age-bent, begging thro' the Streets
> Of Babylon, led by a child; his tears run down his beard.
>
> (K729)

The city, then, is for Blake a living spiritual entity. He called the interior London 'Golgonooza', from the root 'golgos', a skull, because the city's existence is in the human brain:

> Golgonooza, the spiritual Four-fold London eternal,
> In immense labours & sorrows, ever building, ever falling.
>
> (K485)

Jerusalem, the heavenly archetype, is described in the Book of Revelation, as 'coming down from heaven', not as realized in time. Striving to realize that archetype laid up in heaven is the time-spirit, Los, who, seeing the vision inwardly, strives against the inertia and evil forces of this world (Babylon is Blake's name for the secular city),

> Here, on the banks of Thames, Los builded Golgonooza,
> Outside the gates of the Human Heart . . .
>
> In fears
>
> He builded it, in rage & in fury. It is the Spiritual Fourfold
> London, continually building & continually decaying desolate.
>
> (K684)

Blake's London is what Henry Corbin has called an 'emblematic city', the never-realized attempt of the collective life of its inhabitants to build the holy city of Jerusalem. Jerusalem can never, in the very nature of time and change be fully realized on earth, yet Jerusalem has, in Golgonooza, her refuges, her 'secret chambers' in the houses of London's inhabitants, and among these Blake's own house in 'lovely Lambeth', where he and his Catherine lived in the early years of their marriage, and where a vine grew unpruned in their small garden. It would be possible—indeed many of these associations have been made by Foster Damon and others—to relate Blake's emblematic London to either private or public associations. So his happy visits to the Linnell family in Hampstead are implicit in his sacred topography:

> The fields from Islington to Marybone,
> To Primrose Hill and Saint John's Wood,
> Were builded over with pillars of gold,
> And there Jerusalem's pillars stood.
>
> . . .
>
> The Jew's-harp-house & the Green Man
> The Ponds where Boys to bathe delight,
> The fields of Cows by Willan's farm
> Shine in Jerusalem's pleasant Sight. (K649–50)

So by contrast we have 'Mournful ever-weeping Paddington' and 'Tyburn's deathful shade' where mere boys were hanged for minor offences against property. As Blake listened to the voices of London he heard much that was terrible—conscription of men as the cannon-fodder of war, industrial enslavement of women and children—all the sufferings and injustices of a society from which Jerusalem—the soul—is 'cast forth'

> . . . upon the wilds to Poplar and Bow,
> To Malden & Canterbury in the delights of cruelty.
> The Shuttles of death sing in the sky to Islington & Pancrass,
> Round Marybone to Tyburn's River, weaving black melancholy as a net,
> And despair as meshes closely wove over the west of London
> Where mild Jerusalem sought to repose in death and be no more.
> (K668)

But Jerusalem found refuge in the humble house of Blake and his wife in Lambeth. There Blake's earliest Prophetic Books were written:

> We builded Jerusalem as a City & a Temple; from Lambeth
> We began our Foundations, lovely Lambeth. O lovely Hills
> Of Camberwell. (K729)

For Blake all cities must reflect the paradigm, the archetype. Blake envisages not only all the 'twenty-eight cities' of England, but cities yet to be, and he names America, where there will be planted 'the seeds of Cities and of Villages in the Human Bosom'. (K728) The 'labour' of all cities must be to realize Jerusalem 'on earth as it is in Heaven':

> O lovely mild Jerusalem! . . .
> I see thy Gates of precious stones, thy Walls of gold & silver.
> Thou art the soft reflected image of the Sleeping Man
> Who, stretch'd on Albion's rocks, reposes amidst his Twenty-
> eight
> Cities, where Beulah lovely terminates in the hills & valleys of
> Albion,
> Cities not yet embodied in Time and Space; plant ye
> The Seeds, O Sisters, in the bosom of Time & Space's womb,
> To spring up for Jerusalem, lovely shadow of Sleeping Albion.
> Why wilt thou rend thyself apart & build an Earthly Kingdom
> To reign in pride & to opress & to mix the Cup of Delusion?
> (K730)

'Beulah' is Blake's symbol (derived from the Bible, by way of Swedenborg) for the state of marriage, the realm of feeling, of a private world of tenderness and kindness where the 'seed' of cities grows, not in the political and public sphere, but within the lives of individuals. Politics cannot build Jerusalem, but only human souls, each individually toiling to realize the heavenly order on earth. Blake's vision was that England should become a 'holy land'. Throughout his Prophetic Books, Albion (the collective national being) is said repeatedly to be 'asleep'—that is to say in a state of unconsciousness of higher things. The 'sleepers' do not build according to the archetype, but solely in terms of material interests, in the lowest of the four 'worlds', that of the Ulro, the material world: Blake saw materialism as 'delusion' because it is oblivious of the higher worlds of the soul's values of feeling (Beulah) and the collective archetype of 'Eden, the Land of Life' in which Blake found his 'supreme delight'.

In contrast with Jerusalem, mother of souls and bride of 'Jesus, the Imagination'—for the soul must be wedded to the spirit—is Babylon, city of this world. Blake's Babylon is the 'cruel' Goddess Nature—the world of generation seen as the supreme and only power. The laws of Babylon understand men and women as no more than their mortal selves. The morality of Jerusalem is based on Imagination, immortal and boundless; Babylon knows only a moral law imposed on the natural man. Imagination can 'distinguish between the man and his present state', for 'men pass on' while 'states' are mere stages on the way.

> Every Harlot was a Virgin once,
> Nor canst thou ever change Kate into Nan. (K771)

Kate and Nan are unique souls, neither harlot nor virgin, which are 'states' Kate or Nan may pass through. In Babylon forgiveness has no such ground, a sinner is a sinner and incurs the punishment of the moral law, which belongs to the natural order. When the spiritual vision closes, then the Mortal Worm 'Brings forth Moral Virtue & the cruel Virgin Babylon', an external code, 'cruel' because it can only condemn and pass judgement. Babylon is always, in Blake's prophetic mythology, called a 'virgin' because she does not receive God in a 'marriage' of love, but is self-righteous, and can only be redeemed when, through reconciliation with Jerusalem, the soul, Jerusalem will 'give her into the arms of God, you Lord and Husband'. The 'virginity' of Babylon is the self-righteousness of moral virtue as against love of the 'Universal Saviour', the God within. Blake continually denounces the 'cruelty' of natural law, the Deism of his day and the 'selfish virtues of the natural heart'.

Babylon is the 'mother of war', the ultimate moral sanction of competing nations: where the kingdom of the Imagination unites, natural morality is self-centred and divisive. In Babylon Jerusalem's love and forgiveness is condemned, as protecting sinners, and Jerusalem becomes 'a wandering harlot in the streets', condemned to suffer in prison, or to labour 'at the mills' where the Soul has no recourse against the powers of this world.

The sole object of all the labours of Golgonooza, 'ever building, ever falling', is to provide an earthly habitation for Jerusalem. It is ever in secrecy and obscurity, in human love, in every sense of that word, that the foundations of the city are laid; and in a passage of great beauty (where, again, Lambeth is invoked) Blake perfectly and eloquently expresses all he felt about what a human city is, in its inner essence, as a building of human souls each individually, and all collectively labouring to embody a vision whose realization will be only when all is done 'on earth as it is in heaven', according to the archetype of the human Imagination. Blake never presented the building of Jerusalem as the work of a few men of outstanding genius or so-called 'originality', but rather of all the city's inhabitants, the 'golden builders':

> What are those golden builders doing? where was the burying-
>   place
> Of soft Ethinthus? near Tyburn's fatal Tree? is that
> Mild Zion's hill's most ancient promontory, near mournful
> Ever weeping Paddington? is that Calvary and Golgotha
> Becoming a building of pity and compassion? Lo!
> The stones are pity, and the bricks, well wrought affections
> Enamel'd with love & kindness, & the tiles engraven gold,
> Labour of merciful hands, the beams & rafters are forgiveness:

The mortar & cement of the work, tears of honesty: the nails
And the screws & iron braces are well wrought blandishments
And well contrived words, firm fixing, never forgotten,
Always comforting the remembrance: the floors, humility:
The cielings, devotion: the hearths, thanksgiving.
Prepare the furniture, O Lambeth, in thy pitying looms,
The curtains, woven tears & sighs wrought into lovely forms
For comfort; there the secret furniture of Jerusalem's chamber
Is wrought. Lambeth! the Bride, the Lamb's Wife, loveth thee.
Thou art one with her & knowest not of self in thy supreme joy.
Go on, builders in hope, tho' Jerusalem wanders far away
Without the gate of Los, among the dark Satanic wheels. (K632)

In contrast with the labours of the Golden Builders in 'mercy, pity, peace and Love' Babylon's city pursues the rigour of judgement and mutual condemnation. Jerusalem is 'cast forth' as

. . . The Shadow of delusions!
The Harlot daughter! Mother of pity and dishonourable
forgiveness! (K640)

Instead of a world based on mutual forgiveness where 'transgressors' [as all are] meet in brotherhood around the table/Or in the porch and garden' natural morality creates a world of hate, of

War and deadly contention Between
Father and Son, and light and love! All bold asperities
Of Haters met in deadly strife, rending the house & garden,
The unforgiving porches, the tables of enmity, and beds
And chambers of trembling & suspition, hatreds of age & youth,
And boy & girl, & animal & herb, & river & mountain,
And city & village, & house & family, That the Perfect
May live in glory, redeem'd by Sacrifice of the Lamb
And of his children before sinful Jerusalem, To Build
Babylon, the City of Vala, the Goddess Virgin-Mother.
She is our Mother! Nature! (K640)

— and Blake raised his lonely prophetic voice:

> I behold Babylon in the opening Streets of London, I behold
> Jerusalem in ruins wandering about from house to house.
> This I behold: the shudderings of death attend my steps.
> I walk up and down in Six Thousand Years: their Events are
> present before me. (K714)

Would he have found it otherwise now?

The City of Golgonooza — of 'work in progress' — is, like the New Jerusalem of St. John's Book of Revelation, fourfold because we are ourselves fourfold. This fourfold archetype has many precedents, in Blake's own case the fourfold Man of the vision of Ezekiel, and the fourfold city of St. John's Apocalypse. In our own century C. G. Jung has familiarized us with the four 'functions' of man as reason, feeling, sensation and intuition. Blake's Four Zoas correspond to Jung's four 'functions'; they are 'four mighty ones' who are in 'every breast', and the mythological action of Blake's Prophetic Books is based on the interplay — the strife and final harmonizing — of the four Living Creatures, ('Zoas') of the Vision of Ezekiel, and St. John.

> The Four Living Creatures, Chariots of Humanity Divine
> Incomprehensible
> In beautiful Paradises expand. These are the Four Rivers of
> Paradise
> And the Four Faces of Humanity, fronting the Four Cardinal
> Points
> Of Heaven, going forward, forward irresistible from Eternity to
> Eternity. (K744)

As the human psyche, so the human city.

Golgonooza, therefore, the Spiritual Fourfold London Eternal takes the form of a mandala; much like that of St. John, with its 'gates' and its sacred precincts. Blake describes that city at great length, but never drew it in diagrammatic form. Foster Damon did so, and it can be found in his *Blake Dictionary*. But this flat diagram cannot accurately represent the three-dimensional city, with each of its four 'gates' themselves fourfold; and the fourfold orientation is endlessly multiplied in every 'inhabitant' and object within the city:

> And every part of the City is fourfold; & every inhabitant
> fourfold.
> And every pot & vessel & garment & utensil of the houses,
> And every house, fourfold: but the third Gate in every one
> Is clos'd as with a threefold curtain of ivory & fine linen &
> ermine. (K633)

The 'Western Gate' – that of the senses – is closed by the 'curtain' of the physical body (the ivory bones and woven fibres of the bodily 'garment') until man's return to Paradise, whose 'Western gate' is closed with Adam's banishment, as told both in Genesis and by Blake's great master, Milton. The reduplication of the gates of Golgonooza and their guardians has the complexity of a Far-Eastern Buddhist diagram: 'Sixty-four thousand Genii guard the Eastern Gate' and the number is repeated for each of the four gates, suggesting an inexhaustible energy at work – for Golgonooza is essentially a 'work in progress', the achievement of human imagination triumphant over surrounding non-entity:

> Around Golgonooza lies the land of death eternal, a Land
> Of pain and misery and despair and ever brooding melancholy.
> (K633)

The City of Golgonooza exists in time and is the labour of men and women in this world to realize the city 'on earth as it is in heaven,' to build the outer city in the image of the inner city or, in the words of the Irish mystic, A.E., to make the 'politics of time' conform to 'the politics of eternity'. Such was Plato's theme, and St. Augustine's, and of Blake's own teacher, Swedenborg; whose 'emblematic city' was, as for Blake, London, the city where he himself lived and taught for many years.

It was Swedenborg, certainly, who was Blake's most immediate and obvious source of his astonishing and rich conception of a city within. Swedenborg called the inner worlds the 'heavens', regions not of 'eternal rest' but of varied activities, with cities, houses, landscapes, dress and all surroundings in 'correspondence' with the states of the spirits themselves. For Swedenborg the 'heavens' and the 'hells' were the habitations of the discarnate, but Blake did not so conceive the City of Golgonooza, which was built in time and space. Swedenborg's London of the spirit-world likewise has a fourfold structure, with people of different, so-to-say, castes, though these are not so fully developed as are Blake's Four Zoas. The account is included in Swedenborg's 'continuation' of *The Last Judgment* (first published in London in 1758). It is characteristic of Swedenborg's dualistic religious attitude (this is a matter on which Blake criticized him) that there are two cities, one for the saved, the other for the damned. And he writes:

> The centre of one of these cities is the meeting-place of merchants which, in the English London, is called the Exchange. There the governors dwell. Above the centre is the east; below it is the west; on the right side is the south; on the left side is the north. In the eastern quarter dwell those who, more than others, live a life of charity. There are magnificent palaces there. In the southern quarter dwell the wise, among whom are many splendid things. In the northern quarter dwell those who, more than others, love freedom of speech and of writing. In the western quarter dwell those who profess faith. (paragraph 42)

The insistence on a geometric structure is characteristic of all such diagrammatic projections of the inner worlds, including of course St. John's Apocalypse; but Swedenborg's abstract diagram is remote indeed from Blake's impassioned topography of his emblematic city of London. In St. John's Holy City the centre is the Tree of Life, and a flowing river; while in the city of Golgonooza the centre is the palace of Los, the time-spirit, surrounded by a moat of fire. There the 'sons of Los' labour at the 'furnaces' where the souls who 'descend' into generation are embodied in space and time. Blake held the Neoplatonic, not the Christian, view, that souls pre-exist and re-incarnation is implicit in his mythology also. His beautiful Arlington Court tempera illustrates in great detail Porphyry's *De Antro Nympharum*, (which describes the descent and return of souls entering and leaving mortal life) and in his writings likewise this view is implicit. Los, 'time' and his 'emanation' Enitharmon (space) are the parents of all those souls who descend into the world of generation: 'The Male is a furnace of Beryll, & the female is a golden loom', – the 'Loom' on which, as in Porphyry, mortal bodies are woven. 'The Sons of Los clothe them & feed & provide houses & fields' (K512) – for with every new birth a new region of experience comes into being, each an unique world; and through the interplay of these unique worlds – for each is, as in Traherne, sole heir to the whole world, since imagination is indivisible – the inner human city is built and sustained.

> And every Generated Body in its inward form
> Is a garden of delight & a building of magnificence
> Built by the Sons of Los . . .
> And the herbs & flowers & furniture & beds & chambers
> Continually woven in the Looms of Enitharmon's Daughters,
> In bright Cathedron's golden Dome with care & love & tears.
>
> (K512)

As for Plotinus, so for Blake, the souls seek generation in order to perfect both themselves and the world; generation is at once something desired, incurred by some imperfection, and chosen in order to labour towards the perfection of the entire world. The generating souls are far from perfect, and Golgonooza itself is imperfect, unlike the archetypal Jerusalem which Golgonooza ever strives to realize. They are 'piteous Passions and Desires/With neither lineament nor form' for whom life in this world is the opportunity of realization; as they 'choose their affinities/So are they born on Earth'. (K512) We may here remember Plato himself, who at the end of the *Republic* describes how the generating souls choose 'patterns of lives' before their descent into generation. Blake's Golgonooza indeed Plato combines elements from St. John, Swedenborg, his readings of Plotinus and Plato himself.

Also from Plato himself and the Neo-Platonists Blake took the idea of the varying degrees of forgetfulness of eternity into which the generating souls fall, as they come to drink the waters of Lethe (matter) on entering this world. Only in the city of Babylon does the more usual Christian idea of sin and punishment prevail—for the rest Blake, like Plotinus, spoke of 'sleep' and 'awakening'. Those Blake calls 'sleepers', 'meer passion and appetite', have no memory of their eternal nature but are totally immersed in bodily existence. Others—and these include (besides the lovers of wisdom in the Platonic sense), the poets, painters, musicians and architects—remember eternal things; or as we might say perceive more clearly the inner realities of the archetypal world of the Imagination. It is these who are above all the agents of the building of Golgonooza according to that pattern 'laid up in heaven', as Plato says—heaven being, in the Gospels also, 'within'. Works of art—copies of the archetype—serve in turn to awaken and remind the 'sleepers' who cannot themselves perceive the 'originals'. Hence the necessity for the arts, not to copy nature or describe experiences of the natural 'mortal worm' but in order that the human race shall never forget our true—that is our spiritual—home, and our spiritual nature. The natural world is not in reality a universe of 'rocks and solids' ('matter' in the modern sense) but, in Blake's words, the 'looking-glass of Enitharmon' in which the 'originals laid up in heaven' are reflected. (The symbol of the mirror is traditional and Blake doubtless found it in the writings of Boehme.

The city of Golgonooza is called the city of human 'Art and Manufacture', not in the modern commercial sense but because the human city exists in order to embody human values and realities. In Golgonooza there are 'mighty Spires & Domes of ivory and gold' embodying visions of the eternal world that for Blake was reality itself. These the Sons of Los labour to embody,

> Creating form & beauty around the dark regions of sorrow,
> Giving to airy nothing a name and a habitation
> Delightful, with bounds to the Infinite putting off the Indefinite
> Into most holy forms of Thought; such is the power of inspiration
> They labour incessant with many tears & afflictions,
> Creating the beautiful House for the piteous sufferer. (K514–5)

When I.A. Richards wrote that 'poetry is the house of the soul' he might have been thinking of Blake, for whom the arts of Imagination are precisely that. Such is the case in the eternal world, but in the world of generation these are replaced by positive activities, which partially reflect and mediate them to those who in this world are spiritually 'asleep' in the Platonic sense:

> ... in Eternity the Four Arts, Poetry, Painting, Music
> And Architecture, which is Science, are the Four Faces of Man.
> Not so in Time & Space: there Three are shut out, and only
> Science remains thro' Mercy, & by means of Science the Three
> Become apparent in Time & Space in the Three Professions,
> Poetry in Religion: Music, Law: Painting, in Physic & Surgery:
> That Man may live upon Earth till the time of his awaking.
> (M.27.55–61. K514)

While the Daughters of Enitharmon toil at their task of 'clothing' the generating souls the Sons of Los labour at the Furnaces

> ... in fury of Poetic Inspiration
> To build the Universe stupendous, Mental forms Creating.
> (K519)

From the cruel laws of nature Imagination is 'the Saviour', opening for the soul another order of things. Imaginative art is the language of this other vision, and the great visions of the world have from time immemorial been embodied in the music, painting, poetry, architecture and the other arts of every civilization. In the absence of this vision a naturalistic art usurps the place of true art, copying from nature; so that the arts themselves, whose function is to embody and communicate realities of the Imagination, themselves becomes degraded:

> Divine Union Deriding, And Denying Immediate Communion with God, The Spoilers say, 'Where are his Works That he did in the Wilderness? Lo, what are these? Whence came they?' These are not the Works of Egypt nor Babylon, Whose Gods are the Powers Of this World, Goddess Nature, Who first spoil & then destroy Imaginative Art; For their Glory is War and Dominion. (K776–7)

An art uninformed by an imaginative vision is but another region of Babylon.

In the City of Imagination there is neither war nor dominion. In the material world if one becomes rich it is at the expense of others who must be poor, since material possessions are divisible. But in the world of Imagination, its regions extend with the number of those who participate – all belongs, not in part, but wholly, to all, like the light of the sun itself. The delight of music of a concert is not divided but multiplied by the number of those who participate in it, and so with the other arts – paintings and poems; the Taj Mahal and the Primavera of Botticelli, and Hamlet and Lear inhabit the minds of thousands without the least diminution of their riches. The inhabitants of Jerusalem are without number, and their treasures are inexhaustible. How can a civilization be measured unless by the wealth and treasuries of the Imagination which it has created?

Blake supremely admired the builders of the great cities of

art—Michelangelo and the other Florentine architects and painters, who were, like the builders of the Gothic cathedrals, working according to the true forms of the Imagination: recognized by all because innate in all. Wren's St. Pauls he admired less, as a temple of reason, falling short of the supreme Imaginative vision. In St. Paul's he saw a monument, rather, to 'natural religion' and the Goddess Nature. He would himself gladly have used his gifts in the public service of his own city, would have liked in Westminster Abbey to make great frescos comparable to those of the great Florentines; but he was never given the opportunity to do this. He was indignant and bitter in his protest against the commercial values of the England of his day where money and not vision was already, then as now, the supreme value in the public domain. He lamented the absence of such enlightened patronage as the Papacy and the Medicis who set the artists of Florence to build and adorn the churches of Italy, where a spiritual vision of mankind's purpose on earth remained paramount. Blake would have liked to 'make England what Italy is, an Envied Storehouse of Intellectual Riches.' (K601) In the Catalogue of his one public exhibition something of Blake's bitterness in the face of his time's apathy in matters of the Imagination for once sounds a note of helplessness:

> The Artist wishes it was now the fashion to make such monuments, and then he should not doubt of having a national commission to execute these two pictures (the spiritual forms of Nelson and Pitt) on a scale that is suitable to the grandeur of the nation, who is the parent of his heroes, in high finished fresco, where the colours would be as pure and as permanent as precious stones, though the figures were one hundred feet in height. (K566)

As it is, Blake's masterpiece—his engravings of the Book of Job—is none the less a national treasure for being executed within inches, not hundreds of feet, for the magnitude of works of Imagination cannot be measured; and these small works have created a region of the England of the Imagination unsurpassed by any, and 'inhabited' by multitudes to whom they are as familiar as any play of Shakespeare or a melody of Handel or Vaughan Williams.

As for Babylon, it is always, for the soul (Jerusalem), a place of exile and servitude. We may live in such a city all our lives but without ever becoming reconciled to the meaningless and the beautiless, the absence of any of those works of the arts of the Imagination which reflect the cosmic order. No phrase of Blake's is better known than 'those dark Satanic Mills', felt, and not without good reason, to be a perfect description of the landscape of the Industrial Revolution. The attribution is even more just than it appears; for these words were not in fact used by Blake to describe the industrial landscape, (which in Blake's lifetime had scarcely yet arisen) but the mentality—the ideology—which gave rise to the landscape, that of mechanistic materialism. Blake identified this current of thought with the names of Bacon, Newton and Locke, names revered in his day and in our own, as the originators of Western materialism and the world that has grown from that deadly and soul-destroying ideology. Satan is called 'The Miller of Eternity' and 'Prince of the Starry Wheels'. Los asks Satan,

Art thou not Newton's Pantocrator, weaving the Woof of Locke?
To Mortals thy Mills seem everything (K483)

—and Los dismisses Satan with the words:

> Thy Work is Eternal Death with Mills & Ovens & Cauldrons.
> Trouble me no more; thou canst not have Eternal Life.
> (K483)

These are not issues to be safely relegated to the sphere of 'history of ideas'—something over and done with, belonging to the ignorant past. On the contrary, whereas scientists and the natural sciences have meanwhile advanced into a universe very different from that mechanistic hell which built the 'dark Satanic Mills', our society is still in the power of its machines, our dehumanizing technology, idols we have ourselves created until, in Blake's words, written of the Giant Albion, 'his machines are woven with his life'.

The typical city of the materialist civilization may meet a certain 'standard of living' in matters of housing, amenities, water-supply, sanitation and the rest, employment, social services, all those things which were the object of Utopian Communism, or of 'the American way of life' with its superabundance of material goods. What is notably lacking in cities built without the vision of the 'heavenly original' is any trace of beauty, where the eyes can rest and find peace or delight. There may be stupendous works in terms of size, productivity, efficiency, but the soul is starved. We never feel at home in the absence of beauty, we wander the streets (an image to which Blake often returns in writing of the soul's lot in Babylon) but never find home. All seek to create about ourselves some small expression of that universal city; we need beauty, 'the bread of sweet thought and the wine of delight', starved in surroundings where none is to be found, where the buildings and surroundings do not reflect the archetype of the ever-present, never-realized pattern of the *sancta civitas*, the pattern of the 'golden builders' be they architects or poets, painters, or musicians. In the *sancta civitas* there are no exiles, for no matter whether it be in Rome, Athens, or some little white timber-built town in New England, we feel instantly happy and at ease there. The expressions and styles of this eternal city are various, but whether it be in some ancient Chinese painting, the sculptures of Athens or of Southern India, Gothic or Renaissance, the world of the Imagination is everywhere our native country.

One other thought I would add. In thinking of examples of beautiful buildings, of beautiful cities, we name as examples, almost without thinking, temples, churches, mosques, the tombs of Christian or Islamic saints or temples of ancient Egypt or Mexico; for there is at the heart of all beauty—and of the archetype inscribed within us by whose means we measure the beautiful—a sacred essence. Those works which most fully satisfy our thirst for beauty always, surely, reflect some vision of the sacred, some spiritual aspiration; cannot, so it seems, be created unless this be so.

When I was young, and, together with my Cambridge contemporaries, more or less influenced by Marxist idealism, we were supposed to admire the then newly-built Battersea power-station. It was the work of one of our best architects, Giles Gilbert Scott, and conceived as an example of architecture embodying the socialist ideal of a Worker State; a totally work-oriented secular society of collective effort towards a materialist Utopia in which all material needs would be satisfied. There was much talk about building beautiful factories for the workers, in those days, and of adorning them with modern art. And yet the utile, however worthy the purpose or technically impressive the construction, has never yet succeeded in creating an architecture that speaks to the imagination in its own language. Blake would surely have seen, in merely decorating factories or machines in themselves expressing material values, a false view of man and his purpose on earth, an evasion of fundamental issues, a merely superficial decoration of the ever-desolate streets of Babylon. Technology does not address the soul, does not speak to, or from, the archetype. We may admire the functional utility of Battersea power-station but we cannot love it; our souls cannot inhabit it, as we can the cathedrals of Durham, or of Chartres, or the temples of Athens or Karnak, or the mosques of Agra or Cordova, or any temple of the gods under whatever name. In the sanctuaries of all cultures we feel at home, we feel a sense of familiarity, whereas in the secular cities of the modern West we feel strangely alien, perpetual exiles. There is a sense of home-coming in all buildings which, in whatever degree, somehow serve or recognize a sacred centre—the cloisters of a monastery or of a College, dependent as these are upon some purpose or value the soul acknowledges; or a library—I think of the Wren Library in Cambridge, or even the British Museum reading-room, whose dome is, in its very geometric form, somehow congenial to the state of intellectual concentration of its occupants; as with any building, however simple, whose purpose is in some way linked to a sacred centre. This may be the hearth to which a family turns – the crofts of the poor in the Western Highlands, or the Irish cabin, or the tepee of the Amerindians, or indeed just any accommodating room where there are a few simple loved objects – photographs, pebbles or shells from some beach, books, tapes of music. Can this be so in a block of high-rise flats? Perhaps even these can shelter the Golden Builders. But it surely remains true that whereas the materialist ideology, against which Blake so set his face, can produce machines of a precision to make us marvel, in its cities we feel perpetual exiles from something that is not reflected back to us by our surroundings, whose absence is ever-present to us.

Suffering according to Blake's Illustrations of Job

I HAVE sometimes thought that the Christian Church has dwelt somewhat morbidly upon the sufferings of Jesus Christ on the Cross, to the exclusion of the transcendent joy of the Resurrection – however one may understand that Mystery. Especially I have been disgusted by a strain of masochism, or sadism, or both, in the Catholic Post-Counter-Reformation cult of the Stations of the Cross. Blake – although in many ways he admired the theocracy of the Catholic Church – specifically objected to what he saw as a worship of the dead body of Jesus Christ:

> He took on Sin in the Virgin's Womb,
> And put it off on the Cross & Tomb
> To be Worship'd by the Church of Rome. (K749)

This excessive dwelling upon the bodily sufferings and death of Jesus is not found in the Greek or Russian Orthodox churches, in which the risen Pantocrator reigns in glory, depicted in the dome, representing the heavens; nor indeed in the great Gothic cathedrals: one may remember the Christ Enthroned over the great West Door of Chartres and many besides. I have been inclined to contrast this Post-Reformation and Counter-Reformation dwelling upon mortal pain and death with the Indian Shiva's dance of immortal life, of life and death as one single cycle.

And yet it can be seen otherwise – that only in the figure of Jesus Christ, whom Blake, following Swedenborg, calls 'the Divine

Humanity', God in human form, are we shown the divine being entering fully into the experience of human suffering. Prince Siddhartha, the enlightened prince who became the Buddha, knew compassion, and taught release from suffering; but if the figure of Jesus is – as I believe – the supreme revelation of the divine nature sacrificing itself, it is because, as man, he knew and transcended total suffering; and is in every human being the divine presence which accepts, and also transcends, suffering and mortality.

Therefore it is that in his great work on suffering, the twenty-two engravings illustrating the Book of Job, made towards the end of his life – in his sixties – Blake chose the theme not of the mystery of the Crucifixion of Jesus, the divine nature, but the sufferings of poor mortal Job, of Everyman confronting the mysteries of God, whom he worshipped and sought to understand, but did not know face to face. Like most of us – all of us – Job is confronting the mystery of being itself, in whose power he is, has never denied, has tried to reach towards, to obey, to understand. Why then has this blameless man to suffer as he does? The Book of Job is indeed the story of Everyman; is not Kafka's K, in *The Trial*, a son of Job? K, if you remember, discovers one day that a trial process has been opened against him: why? Of what, and by whom, is he accused? Poor K feels himself to be utterly blameless; so did Job. Is God then a monster of wanton cruelty? Jung – who as a doctor, a healer, is on Job's side – does see in God a mixture of all qualities, good and evil. Jung on the whole takes the view that Job's was the better character, that suffering mortal Everyman could teach God a lesson or two. There have been times when many of us have felt the same impulse to challenge a God who has made things as they are. Somewhere Elias Canetti – like Kafka, a Jew – has written that the Last Judgment will be when humanity rises up and judges God. Well, maybe; there are different levels, heights and depths real enough to those who are in them. But only in what Blake has called the 'supreme state' do we see things as they are; the rest are 'states that are not, but ah! seem to be.'

Suffering, for Blake is a state of ignorance – ignorance, that is, of God; who is, for Blake the God within. In the Churches Blake saw the God of this World – the God of the moral law – worshipped; the way to discover the Divine Humanity is not through morality and observance but by spiritual rebirth.

Such is the secret of liberation; to England's Everyman he says he should 'leave mortal things': 'then would he arise from his Grave, then he would meet the Lord in the Air & then he would be happy'. Blake sees happiness as our proper state, within reach of all who are prepared to 'leave mortal things' for the kingdom of the Divine Humanity. Suffering, for Blake – who knew much suffering in his own life and saw much in his own war-afflicted world – is not, as some would have it, a state of final wisdom, a heroic recognition of things as they are. No, the supreme state is happiness, and Blake uses the English equivalent of the Indian word, *ananda*, 'bliss'.

> And trees & birds & beasts & men behold their eternal joy.
> Arise, you little glancing wings, and sing your infant joy!
> Arise, and drink your bliss, for every thing that lives is holy!
>
> (K195)

What, then, of the sufferings of Job? Here it must be said that there is no question of whether or not Blake correctly interpreted the intentions of the author of the Book of Job, or whether his understanding conforms either with Christian or Jewish orthodoxy. In fact there have been both Christian and Jewish commentators who have shared Blake's view that Job was not a figure of innocence exposed to sufferings wantonly inflicted, because, in Jung's words, Satan had a bet with God. There have been many others who have taken many different views. To Blake, then, Job was not, as for Jung, God's moral superior: he was, on the contrary, blinded by self-righteousness, to Blake of all things the most abhorrent. A virtuous selfhood – a virtuous and self-righteous ego – is the contrary of the Divine Humanity, and as he calls the one Jesus, the Imagination, so he names the other, unambiguously, Satan, the Selfhood. Thus the parts cast for the drama enacted by Job (and re-enacted in all ages) are Satan, the Selfhood, the human ego, and the indwelling Divine Humanity. In addition to these we have Job's wife, his *anima*, his soul-image. Here Blake changes the Bible story, in which Job's wife fails him and is replaced, in the end of the drama, by another and presumably better, wife. But Blake, thinking no doubt of his own faithful Catherine, makes her the sharer of all Job's sufferings, of his enlightenment, and his final happiness. Besides these, there are Job's three friends, and the young man, Elihu; who correspond, in Blake's own symbolic mythology, to the Four Zoas, the 'four mighty ones who are in every breast'. Thus in Blake's setting-forth of the story of Job it is an inner experience, an inner drama, that we are witnessing. Jung has gone so far as to suggest that even events of the outer world are, properly understood, events of the soul; Blake shared this view, 'body is a portion of soul discerned by the five senses.' (I mention this here, in passing, lest it should be objected that Blake's is an escapist view. But if even events of the outer world are deemed to mirror events of the soul and not vice versa as our materialist orthodoxy supposes) then we cannot make a distinction between inner and outer. What, such objectors might say, about 'real' suffering—wars, cancer, poverty and economic conditions? Real indeed: but, Blake would answer (and so would every spiritual tradition),

> . . . every Natural Effect has a Spiritual Cause, and Not
> A Natural; for a Natural Cause only seems: it is a Delusion
> Of Ulro. (K513)

What about bombs then? In that context Jung has pointed out what an extremely powerful and dangerous cause the human psyche is: bombs and the rest of those modern marvels of technology don't happen in the course of nature: human beings make bombs, they do not just make themselves in test-tubes. Not natural causes but human choice has made these things; collective choice it may be but we cannot for that reason dissociate ourselves from it.

But again I digress: in Blake's telling of the story of Job we have the story of an inner event; an event within the soul of the old Biblical character of Job, but also, for Blake, above all and specifically, a drama he saw being enacted in the collective soul of the English nation, the Giant Albion. Blake was concerned above all to deliver his prophetic message to his own nation – to us. That message is indeed universal, but it is also specific. In my book *The Human Face of God* I have set forth the many parallels between the visual symbolic depictions of the drama of Job, and the text of the Prophetic Books. Blake's diagnosis of the sickness and suffering of Job is not different from his diagnosis of the 'sickness of Albion' – the spiritual sickness of the English nation under the domination of the materialist philosophy imposed by the rationalist ego, oblivious of spiritual causes.

In any case, I shall follow the order of the twenty-two engravings, although describing I fear only a small fragment of their rich content. Of their visual beauty I will say nothing – that you may wonder at for yourselves, while reflecting perhaps that this beauty is not unconnected with the sacred vision that Blake is seeking with all his skill as an engraver to communicate.

The title-page reads, 'Illustrations of the Book of Job', whose title is given both in English and in Hebrew. A flight of seven winged spirits supports the title and these signify the *elohim*, the seven spirits of God whom Christians know as the sevenfold Holy Spirit, Cabalists as the seven lower Sephiroth (the Trinity, completing the Sephirotial number ten, are in the uncreated world). Thus at the outset Blake proclaims in a symbol his belief in spiritual causes; 'Nature is a vision of the Science of the Elohim', he wrote in the poem *Milton*. Each spirit is in turn active on each of the days of creation – the theme is taken up magnificently on Plate 14. Six of the spirits on the title-page show their faces; the seventh turns away, its face averted; why?

In Blake's work no detail is accidental: his seventh spirit has not yet come, the Creation is incomplete, for the kingdom of the Divine Humanity has not yet been established, in Jesus Christ. This sets the scene for the drama of Job's search for the face of God – the human face of God.

With Plate 1, the human actors in the story appear; a dignified family portrait of Job in his prosperity, with his wife and his seven sons and three daughters, his flocks of sheep grazing in the background. Job and his wife sit side by side, the Holy Books open before them; but a marginal text below reads, 'The Letter Killeth, The Spirit giveth life.' Job and his family live by the letter of the law. On the great Tree of Life which shelters them, hang musical instruments, unused – the spiritual gifts which they have neglected, while following the letter of the law. However, outwardly all is well.

In Plate 2 we are shown the inner aspect of things, which is somewhat different. Blake follows Tradition in depicting three levels – the natural, the psychological, and the celestial. Enthroned in the celestial world is God; who, being the God within Job himself, has Job's features, only more radiant. With downpointing finger he summons Satan, who is the central figure in the middle world – the psychological, the world of Job's inner life. In this world are four figures (Satan being the fourth) whom we may equate with the Four Zoas, the 'four mighty ones' who are 'in every breast' (so Blake describes them). We know that Satan is, in the drama of Albion, specifically identified with fallen – natural – reason, responsible, in Blake's view, for the rebellion of the human selfhood against the divine world. There too we see the troubled human faces of Job and his wife, as they behold the arrival of Satan in an enveloping flame. Below, in the natural world, the dignified repose of the first plate is broken; the sons and daughters watch, troubled, as two angels show Job a scroll, the same that in the higher world is being unrolled before God: the record of his life. Job, startled, holds up the Book of the Law, as if defending himself against some challenge, or accusation: has he not kept the law? Why, then, this Day of Reckoning? He is, he protests, blameless.

In the Plate 3, things have gone from bad to worse; the black winged figure of Satan scatters fire and destruction as the house collapses about Job's sons and daughters – as told in the Bible. But for Blake Job's loss of his sons and daughters is not a natural but a spiritual death – the only death Blake recognized. Our children are dead to us when we cease to love them; we cease to love them when we pass moral judgements upon them, and we pass moral judgments when we live by the letter of the law. The spirit of Jesus, we remember, is 'the continual forgiveness of sins', but Job has not yet learned that the spirit of the living God is other than the letter of the law by which he has hitherto lived. 'The letter killeth', Blake had engraved on Plate 1; in Plate 3 we see precisely that – the letter is killing Job's family.

That this is Blake's meaning is clearly enough stated in many passages of the Prophetic Books, with the Giant Albion in the part of Job. Indeed it is clear that the figure of Albion is to a great extent derived from the Book of Job; and when he made his engravings – his supreme work – the story of Albion in turn became a source on which he drew in telling the story of Job. First, by losing contact with the spiritual world, he loses his children:

> His inward eyes closing from the Divine Vision, & all
> His children wandering outside, from his bosom fleeing away
> (K279)

They become externalized as, losing the divine vision, Albion falls into the mentality which sees the world and others as outside himself, not as 'one family' in the Imagination. In a passage full of echoes from the Book of Job Albion laments that his flocks and herds, his fields and hills, his whole world, is lost to him;

His Children exil'd from his breast pass to and fro before him,
His birds are silent on his hills, flocks die beneath his branches,
His tents are fall'n, his trumpets and the sweet sound of his harp
Are silent on his clouded hills that belch forth storms & fire.
(K641)

Blake paints a terrible picture of family harmony giving place to confusion and hatred through Albion's submission to the morality of 'natural religion', the religion of Satan the selfhood:

But father now no more,
Nor sons, nor hateful peace & love, nor soft complacencies,
With transgressors meeting in brotherhood around the table
Or in the porch or garden. No more the sinful delights
Of age and youth, and boy and girl, and animal and herb,
And river and mountain, and city & village, and house & family,
Beneath the Oak & Palm, beneath the Vine & Fig-tree,
In self-denial! – But War and deadly contention Between
Father and Son, and light and love! All bold asperities
Of haters met in deadly strife, rending the house & garden,
The unforgiving porches, the tables of enmity, and beds
And chambers of trembling & suspition, hatreds of age & youth,
And boy & girl & animal & herb, & river & mountain,
And city & village and house & family (K640)

Such is the situation of Job, his world no longer beautiful to him or his family dear.

In Plate 4 Job and his wife sit alone in their ruined world as the messenger brings his news of death and destruction; above is the figure of Satan who now dominates the scene – the human ego, neither more nor less. This too is a traditional view in Christian mystical literature: Satan is not outside us, but within us. 'Every man is born a spectre or Satan', Blake declares, 'and needs a new selfhood continually.' It is the human ego who rebels against the divine order, offering the natural man autonomy – freedom. Milton's Satan declares, 'Better to rule in hell than serve in Heaven' – words many have responded to – Hell being of course by definition the kingdom cut off from God. In terms of the inner life, the divine kingdom is the Imagination, the kingdom of Jesus; that of Satan, the natural world, in which the empirical ego is Lord of This World – according to one of Satan's traditional names.

In Plate 5 we are again shown the state – the new state – of Job's inner universe. In the celestial world the enthroned figure of God has become drowsy and the light of the spiritual sun which emanates from the God within is dimmed and darkened. A company of angels who surround the throne recoils, as the energetic figure of Satan intervenes between the spiritual universe and Job in the natural world below. A cloud is closing in, shutting off the divine world from the natural world, where Job and his wife sit, destitute, in a bare stony landscape. But Job, ever-righteous, is giving to a crippled beggar led by a dog what may be a loaf of bread, or may be a stone; either way there is no joy in the aspects either of giver or of receiver: charity, Blake knew, could be a very cold thing. We may remember in the *Songs of Experience*, 'Holy Thursday':

> Is this a holy thing to see
> In a rich and fruitful land,
> Babes reduc'd to misery
> Fed with cold and usurous hand? (K211)

He has still bitterer words to say elsewhere about those who

> Compell the poor to live upon a Crust of bread, by soft mild arts.
> . . .
> With pomp give every crust of bread you give; with gracious cunning
> Magnify small gifts; reduce the man to want a gift, & then give with pomp. (K323)

Blake was not perhaps impressed by Job's own account of his many charities, God being the only giver.

In Plate 6 we see only the dark earth that Job now inhabits, with stone altars in the background, a ruin, a stone tomb. Satan stands above the now prostrate Job, pouring arrows and flames upon him; the text illustrated is the smiting of Job with boils. His sufferings are no longer circumstantial only, they are now in himself. But, again, Blake interprets the 'boils' in Job's body not as a natural affliction but as a disease of his soul; they are guilt and sin, inflicted upon the man who lives by the letter of a law that condemns sin but knows nothing of forgiveness. Again turning to the parallel of the Giant Albion, we are told what Blake understood by the boils which afflicted Job; Albion laments:

> The disease of Shame covers me from head to feet. I have no
> hope.
> Every boil upon my body is a separate & deadly Sin.
> Doubt first assail'd me, then Shame took possession of me.
> Shame divides Families, Shame hath divided Albion in sunder.
> First fled my Sons & then my Daughters, then my Wild
> Animations,
> My Cattle next, last ev'n the Dog of my Gate; the Forests fled,
> The Corn-fields & the breathing Gardens outside separated,
> The Sea, the Stars, the Sun, the Moon, driv'n forth by my
> disease.
> All is Eternal Death unless you can weace a chaste
> Body over an unchaste Mind! (K643)

But 'the costly Robes of Natural Virtue' are no disguise for 'Spiritual forms without a Veil.' Hypocrisy is not chastity. Blake with his bold realism knew that

> No individual can keep these Laws, for they are death
> To every energy of man and forbid the springs of life.
> (K662)

The passage then continues with the description (already quoted) of the flight of Albion's sons and daughters, the loss of his cattle and wealth, and ends with a return to the theme of guilt and unchastity.

Job is now experiencing in himself those self-searchings and self-condemnations his search for individual natural righteousness has brought upon him. To Blake self-righteousness is the worst, perhaps the only unforgiveable sin.

In the Plate 7 Job's friends arrive, representatives of the Jewish law, who bring him little comfort by insisting that since he is suffering he must have sinned, for suffering is a punishment for sin. Job must necessarily have broken the law, either he or his children; for according to the Mosaic teaching prosperity and happiness reward those who keep the commandments of God. Job still insists that he is absolutely guiltless, and he believes this to be true. In the Plate 8 we see depicted the great protest of man against the human lot: 'Let the Day perish wherein I was born', Job cries; he feels himself to be the victim of meaningless and undeserved affliction. And it is at this point, as those who have read Jung's *Answer to Job* will remember, that Jung is won over by Job's argument: God should not, surely, treat his creature man so cruelly. It is a protest that runs through Jewish literature to the present day. I think of the stories of Isaac Bashevis Singer; especially of one entitled *The Blasphemer*, which tells of the rebel of a village community who accuses God of his unforgiveable cruelty to men and women; and to dumb innocent animals. Hard to answer. After the holocaust what answer indeed has God to give His people? Blake must have been aware of the depth of Job's questioning, and below Plate 8 the words are written:

> And they sat down with him upon the ground seven days and seven nights and none spoke a word unto him for they saw that his grief was very great. (Job II:13)

What but silence can respond to the presence of man's total affliction? Job's friends were not insensitive to his grief.

In the Plate 9 the impasse is broken, as so often in life, not by any answer being found in terms of the situation as it is presented, as it seems to the sufferer himself, but in the form of a startling intervention from another level of consciousness, in the form of a dream. This happens to us also – some terrifying, awe-inspiring or shocking dream does not so much resolve a situation which seems to have no solution, as introduce another element into that situation. This dream is a vision of God, experienced not by Job himself but by one of his friends, Eliphas the Temanite. The awe, terror and authenticity of that dream reaches us still, in the words of the narrator:

> In thoughts from the visions of the night, when deep sleep falleth on man, fear came upon me, and trembling, which made all my bones to shake.
>
> Then a spirit passed before my face; the hair of my flesh stood up: It stood still, but I could not discern the form thereof: an image was before mine eyes, there was silence, and I heard a voice, saying
>
> Shall mortal man be more just than God? Shall a man be more pure than his maker? Behold, he put no trust in his servants; his angels he charged with folly. (Job IV: 13–15)

This great dream carries conviction to our century, who have discovered what all spiritual civilizations have known – that dreams are sent us from levels of consciousness normally inaccessible to us, beyond and above the reality the empirical ego has constructed for itself on a basis of information from the five senses categorized and compared by natural reason. The Bible gives many examples of dreams treated as valid symbolic revelations from these inner worlds. In Blake's awesome illustration we see Eliphas telling his dream, as the numinous presence stands before the sleeper. Eliphas, seated on the ground (the natural world, as symbolized pictorially) points upwards into the world of his dream. Job and his wife, startled, draw apart as they look up, imaginatively, into another man's vision—for the visions of others can often bring enlightenment from that inner invisible universe all share. Job is no longer telling his own story, defending himself, proving himself in the right: he has seen something he had not taken into account, a mystery beyond his reckoning.

In Plate 10, in which his three friends become his three accusers, Job makes, as it were, his last stand; his appeal to God; his aspect is that of supplication, of prayer; he has nothing more to say. Everyone is against him now—even his wife's aspect and attitude seems to suggest that here she is giving him her terrible advice, to 'curse God, and die.'

In all art I know of no depiction of suffering more awe-inspiring than Plate 11. In it Job is alone; as we are each alone in the darkest hour. Hitherto his wife had been beside him, sharing his ordeal; but now he has passed into a place where none can accompany him into his desolation. Instead of his three friends three fiends in the fires of hell seek to drag him down with a chain into the abyss. He lies prostrate on his sleeping mat—for this is an experience of the solitude of night—while over him hovers the figure of Satan, with cloven foot and entwined by the serpent; Satan is in the likeness of God, bearded and venerable, his face cruel as he points to the Book of the Law, while the thunderings and lightnings of Sinai surround the God of This World, the Accuser, in his final triumph over Job, prostrate, helpless, and condemned. Job averts his face and with his hands tries to ward off this terrible realization of the nature of the God whom he has worshipped—the God of This World, of that 'natural religion' against which Blake fought his lifelong battle. It is Satan, in Blake's view—Satan the Selfhood, the reasoner and the accuser, who writes the moral law Job has so religiously kept. In the margin above is written 'Satan himself is transformed into an Angel of Light, & his Ministers into Ministers of Righteousness'; and below 'The triumph of the wicked is short, and the joy of the hypocrite is but for a moment'.

Such is Blake's lifelong theme: the moral law, when uninformed by spiritual understanding is hypocritical and cruel. It is not the law of the Holy Spirit; the religion of Jesus, Blake says, is continual forgiveness of sin. Blake declared himself 'a worshipper of Jesus', the divine humanity, the Imagination that redeems from the law, that forgives continually. This plate is the turning-point in the story of Job as told by Blake; and in the remaining ten plates Blake sets forth another picture of reality than that of Deism – natural religion – of the spiritual world and its nature and its laws. In 'this world' – so called also by Jesus in the Gospels – men and women are subject to the laws of natural morality – the Mosaic law. Blake seeks to show that in our inner worlds things are otherwise.

The stillness, the calm, the promise of hope, one can almost say, the silence depicted in Plate 12, the release from suffering, contrasts with the nightmare and claustrophobic horror of the preceding plate. If a picture was ever a true icon, communicating the hope it depicts to whoever contemplates it, it is this. And if a work of art can heal the human spirit – and for what other purpose do works of sublime art exist – this engraving, but a few square inches in size, surely brings inexhaustible, boundless healing. I have had a copy on my desk for years and yet every time I look at it, it overwhelms me; as does that wonderful passage in Dante – and perhaps Blake was thinking of it – when from the bottom of hell's ever-narrowing circles, from under Satan's hairy thighs, Dante, half carried by Virgil, emerges through a narrow passage in a kind of rebirth, into the stillness and faint light of dawn. In Blake's engraving also dawn is about to break for Job. He is seated, listening now, his three friends beside him, listening too. His wife – his soul – is bowed, still terrified by the experience undergone. In the still dark sky are wonderful stars; and a new figure is entering the scene, the young man Elihu. He is beautiful, as with his outstretched right hand he makes toward the seated group (Job and his wife and his friends) a gesture of refutal, and with his left hand he points upwards; he advances eagerly, like a messenger. The wisdom of experience, of tradition, of the law, as represented by the three friends, has failed;

the young man, Elihu, is the spirit of prophecy, ever-young. It is he who comes, as he claims, to 'speak for God.'

Elihu corresponds – there are many parallels which cannot be developed here – to Blake's own figure of Los, the 'eternal prophet', spirit of inspiration, the fourth Zoa, of whom Blake writes that he 'kept the divine vision in time of trouble'. Blake often seems to identify himself with Los; for the poetic and prophetic genius are one. Elihu is Los, he is the prophet, he is the poetic vision. Perhaps Elihu provided Blake with his model for Los; and again, in these late engravings, all that Los had become in Blake's imagination, comes to enrich, in its turn, the beautiful and eloquent figure of Elihu.

Commentators both Jewish and Christian differ in their view of the part played by Elihu in the Book of Job. According to some, he adds little to the argument; others even suggest that he is an interpolation. If so, such an interpolation must have been made in response to a felt need. For Blake he is central; he does indeed perform the prophetic role, and 'speaks for God', as he claims. His first words claim that he is come to speak 'in God's stead'; but he at once disclaims any personal superiority. He is not, he hastens to say, different from other men: 'I also am formed of the clay.' His claim to speak for God is either presumption (as it has seemed to some commentators) or it is true: Blake held it to be true. Elihu several times repeats his claim:

> Suffer me a little, and I will shew thee that I have yet to speak on God's behalf.
>
> I will fetch my knowledge from afar, and will ascribe righteousness to my maker.
>
> For truly my words shall not be false: he that is perfect in knowledge is with you. (Job XXXVI: 2–4)

An interpolation? A young man's conceit? To believe so is to deny the reality of the prophetic inspiration, and, virtually, to vindicate natural knowledge as against the mystery of God. In earlier chapters we have heard the wisdom of experience from the three friends; now inspiration speaks.

The truth of the claim of Elihu—and of Blake's own claim for inspiration—supposes the reality of a transpersonal mind, a holy spirit in man that 'knoweth all things.' This claim modern views of man—such as C. G. Jung's—are more prepared to consider than was the assured rationalism of the last century, to which such a claim would have been meaningless. Even now there is a tendency to psychologize spiritual mystery, to attribute to 'the unconscious'—a human category—what Tradition sees as the world of God; of the God Within, to be sure, but the within also is transcendent, even though some schools of psychology are reluctant to admit this.

The many sources, the many parallels, in both Jewish and Islamic literature, of Blake's figure of the beautiful youthful visitant I cannot here describe, but Elihu makes the claim of all inspiration, as against what Blake has elsewhere called 'aged ignorance':

> I said, Days should speak, and multitude of years should teach wisdom.
>
> But there is a spirit in man: and the inspiration of the Almighty giveth them understanding. (Job XXXII:7–8)

It is Elihu who plainly tells Job that he has been in the wrong in seeking to justify himself; instead of thinking about himself and proclaiming his own virtue he should have been thinking about God. The God whom Job has served hitherto is the moral God, a construction of the human ego—of Satan the selfhood. How passionately Blake himself held this view is clear from many passages throughout his writings:

'Moral virtues do not exist', he wrote; and

> We do not find any where that Satan is Accused of Sin; he is only accused of Unbelief & thereby drawing Man into Sin that he may accuse him. Such is the Last Judgment—a

> deliverance from Satan's Accusation. Satan thinks that Sin is displeasing to God; he ought to know that Nothing is displeasing to God but Unbelief & Eating of the Tree of Knowledge of Good & Evil. (K615)

– and again,

> It is not because Angels are Holier than Men or Devils that makes them Angels, but because they do not expect Holiness from one another but from God only. (K616)

Job in his steadfastness will be rewarded by a vision of the true living God, of whom Elihu now speaks.

Elihu speaks first of dreams as a source of knowledge of God; thus lifting the discussion from the order of reason to the order of revelation. Blake has engraved in the margins of Plate 12:

> For God speaketh once yea twice, & Man perceiveth it not.
>
> In a Dream, in a Vision of the Night, in deep Slumberings upon the bed
>
> Then he openeth the ears of Man & sealeth their instruction.
>
> That he may withdraw Man from his purpose & hide Pride from Man.
>
> If there be with him an Interpreter, One among a Thousand then he is gracious unto him & saith Deliver him from going down into the Pit. (Job XXXIII: 14–18)

How many psychiatrists have credentials to meet such a claim? Jung himself surely, and others perhaps. One hopes so.

Elihu makes great claims: Job shall see God for himself: 'and he shall see his face with joy: for he will render unto a man his righteousness'. The true God is not the Accuser, but the healer, the source of 'righteousness'. Job's righteousness had not been the righteousness of God; Elihu reproaches him precisely for having said 'I am righteous' and then 'It profiteth a man nothing that he should delight himself with God'. Yet delighting in God is the chief good, the sole end of any human life, God being not simply 'good' but the Good itself. Job's prayer at the beginning of his tribulations was to find God in order to justify himself, to argue his case, like Kafka's K. But at the end his prayer is 'That which I see not teach me to see.'

At this central moment in the drama, we should perhaps pause to ask ourselves whether Blake's interpretation of the cause of suffering is adequate. Is the nature of suffering, its root cause, the sense of guilt, the accusations and counter-accusations of those who inflict and those who sustain these condemnations, who condemn others and ultimately condemn and hate ourselves? I believe that many psychologists would say that a deep-rooted and destructive sense of guilt, projected upon others or suffered in ourselves, is indeed a principle cause of psychological suffering. But what of physical suffering, or physical disease? For these we are surely not to blame. This is indeed a great mystery; accidents, loss of limbs, or sight, these things seem inexplicable. And yet we know so little of physical disease. 'Body is that portion of soul perceived by the five senses' Blake wrote; and if body be 'a portion of soul' may not physical disease be subject to laws similar to those of mental suffering? In some cases this seems clearly to be the case—the medical profession would not deny it. Jesus himself healed a man unable to walk by saying 'your sins are forgiven.' And what of the accident-prone—there are many questions unanswered, or even not yet asked.

On the other side, it is also true that the blind, the physically handicapped, the mentally retarded, are not by any means always the most unhappy people: sometimes the reverse seems to be true. But I am not here to argue Blake's case that the root of suffering lies in the ego which has cut itself off from the God within, but only to state it. 'Bliss' Blake saw as an attribute of life, not circumstantial.

As one magnificent plate follows another the divine mystery-play unfolds. On Plate 13, which illustrates the words: 'then the Lord answered Job out of the Whirlwind', Job and his wife do see God face to face. In Plate 2, God was present in the celestial world but not perceived directly by Job in the natural world. Here there are no longer any barriers; Job sees God face to face; as Blake had claimed 'to converse daily as man with man' with the Divine Humanity, the God Within. Circumstances are not changed, but we are changed. The cause of suffering is within ourselves, and so is its cure.

Here I would like to digress for a moment to speak about the Whirlwind. I need not remind you, in a Christian church, of the Pentecostal vision of the descent of the Holy Spirit upon the disciples as a mighty rushing wind. Wind, or breath, as a symbol of the Holy Spirit, is to be found throughout the Old and the New Testaments and indeed throughout the world. Think of Shelley's West Wind, to whom he prayed 'Make me thy lyre, even as the forest is', and countless other passages of poetry. But there may be more to this central experience of Job. Last year I visited India for the first time; and I had the honour to be introduced to the Master of the famous Sikh monastery at Beas, in the North Punjab. This Master teaches a form of yoga ancient in India which consists in listening to the sound of the universe. This is known to all traditions, he told me; 'some call it the music of the spheres; some call it the wind; others the Holy Spirit', 'we call it sound' – the creative sound to which all is attuned. Wind is an image of the Holy Spirit used in the story of Pentecost. I said that I had always taken that story of the descent of the Holy Ghost as a rushing wind figuratively; no, he said; it is a spiritual reality experienced by whoever attains it. Had the author of the Book of Job known this? Had Blake? I leave you merely to reflect that spiritual knowledge is not a matter of information, but of epiphany; and release from suffering can only result from a change of consciousness.

The vision of God in Plate 13 is followed, in Plate 14, by a vision of the creation in all its glory, in the three worlds. In the margins the six days of creation are depicted; and the engraving itself—the seventh day—is entitled 'when the morning Stars sang together & all the Sons of God shouted for Joy.' The theme is epiphany itself; for creation is completed in mankind's vision of God as the Divine Humanity. This is the arrival of the human kingdom, in which the work of creation is completed. We remember here the title-page showing the seven *elohim*, the creators; the averted face of the seventh spirit has been revealed to Job as the face of humanity. Throughout the series, the face of God is always identical with the face of Job: not because Job has invented a God in his own image but because man is made in the image and likeness of God; as told in the Book of Genesis humanity is a manifestation of the God within; every human face, however obscured, is one among the innumerable faces of God.

Plate 15 shows Behemoth and Leviathan. These are enclosed within a sphere—the time-world, as we may discover, again, from comparison of the design with passages in the text of the Prophetic Books. They represent duality—an aspect of this world which has troubled many besides Job, and Blake himself: good and evil, the light and the dark contraries, which seem to be in the very nature of things, in this world. The finger of God points down to Behemoth and Leviathan the great eternal contraries, while Job, his wife and his three friends look down in awe, from the world of the soul, where they now are aware of the presence of God in the spiritual world above the Soul, into the world of generation where 'without contraries there is no progression.' What we call good and evil are necessary and inseparable, in this world. Unity is only in God.

Plate 16 shows the fall of Satan into the flames of the abyss. Once more we are looking into the inner worlds. In his fall Satan the great Selfhood is accompanied by two other figures, a man and a woman. These are the selfhoods of Job and his wife, now cast off. We have each our own selfhood; Blake often addressed his, as 'my Satan'—'Truly, my Satan, thou art but a dunce', and so on. The

Living God is now again on his throne, and around him, in the radiance of his light, the spiritual sun, a group of cherubs, or children. Nor are these merely angelic decoration: no, for if we look closely we see that the two principle winged children, boy and girl, who seem to be weeping, in penitence, correspond, again, to Job and his wife, whose selfhoods have been cast off into the abyss. They are spiritually new-born, 'as little children' in the kingdom of God. Three others are grouped together: Job's friends, they also spiritually reborn. There is yet another child, haloed, half-hidden behind the figure of the Father: this surely is the Christ-child, promised to the human world by the Jehovah of the Bible, and born, so Blake believed, as Jesus, the Divine Humanity. This I should like to recall, honouring his memory, was pointed out to me by that great follower and scholar of Blake, Kerrison Preston; whose collection of Blake material was left to the Westminster City Library.

Plate 17 shows the human figure of God blessing Job and his wife; while in the margin there is text after text from the Fourth Gospel: 'I and the Father are One'; 'At that day ye shall know that I am in my Father & you in me & I in you'; 'If you loved me ye would rejoice because I said I go unto the Father'—the Christian promise of immortality proclaimed by St. John the Evangelist. The vision of the coming Messiah—who for Blake is Jesus, the Divine Humanity—is the resolution of Job's suffering and the meaning of his words 'I have heard thee with the hearing of my Ear, but now my Eye seeth thee.' This plate is a proclamation of the Swedenborgian doctrine of the 'Divine Humanity' as the only God, as Blake also believed.

Jung, surely, overlooked that affirmation, which Blake understood in the sense of the vision of the God within. Jung thought that Job had won the argument, and at the end thought it best to say no more to a God incapable of speaking his language. But according to the text Job had 'seen' God; he had understood something he had not previously understood, and which brought his sufferings to an end. His consciousness had been transformed, 'and God blessed the latter end of Job more than the beginning'. Strange that Jung, who saw the goal of the individuation process as a discovery of the true Self, should have been so carried away by his advocacy of Job in his self-justification as to have missed so essential a statement of the very goal he himself understood as the goal of human life.

In Plate 18 we see Job praying for his friends; and in Plate 19 a happy contrast with Plate 5, in which a joyless Job gives a loaf or a stone to a joyless beggar. Plate 19 illustrates Job and his wife receiving their guests as for a celebration. The women are wearing their best dresses, their jewels, and their hair elegantly arranged. The text below is 'Everyone also gave him a piece of money.' They also bring as gifts (as in the Scriptural text) earrings—purely non-utilitarian adornments, worn as tokens of that Oriental splendour and magnificence in which human delight in life is expressed; Western puritanism would hardly have brought Job personal adornments, but the divine treasury—'gold of Eden'—is inexhaustible. Job has learned to receive; learned that *he* is not necessarily the giver, congratulating himself on his generosity. Now he understands that from everyone we meet, we receive. This is a joyous scene, as Job and his wife sit under a great fig-tree while behind them is a field of ripening corn. Their world has come to life again.

In Plate 20 Job sits with his three daughters, embracing them: had he learned to value the feminine, to accept woman's love formerly rejected as sin? There is nothing in the text of the Bible to support such an interpretation, but it seems clear that this was what Blake thought. Woman's love was one of those 'sins' that afflicted Job with 'boils'; the notion that 'woman's love is sin' is one against which Blake himself waged his battle; and below the plate we see feminine figures carrying and scattering flowers, the 'loves and graces of eternity.' And to complete this happy conclusion we are shown again, on the last plate, the same family group as in the first, Job and his wife under the great Tree of Life. But now they are not reading the Book of the Law, they have taken down from the tree those musical instruments, and one can almost hear Vaughan Williams's glorious music as one looks at those trumpets and flutes, Job's harp, and the lyre and song-scores of his daughters. The words below—paralleling the earlier text, 'The letter killeth, the spirit giveth life'—are the words 'In burnt Offerings for Sin thou hast no Pleasure.' Job's burnt offerings had been the torments and ultimately the self-torments, of sin according to the laws of the God of This World. What *is* pleasing to God is that every human being should live creatively, from that 'intellectual fountain' which is the holy spirit within each.

The Apocalypse – Blake and Michelangelo

In DIFFERENT ages the theme of the Apocalypse of St. John's Revelation has been differently conceived in the imagination of the Christian Church. In Blake's words, 'its Vision is seen by the [Imaginative Eye] of Every one according to the situation he holds'. (K604) These words already indicate Blake's own understanding of this event, which he conceived not as foreknowledge of future history but as 'vision' of an abiding spiritual reality. It is an archetype; one of those 'stupendous visions' or 'images of wonder' – to use Blake's terms – which do not belong to the temporal order although they will of necessity be reflected in it from time to time. To see the Last Judgement, or Apocalypse, therefore, as a historic event in secular terms is to misconceive its nature. The majority of humankind, as Blake knew very well, have so misconceived it, the natural order (already in Blake's own lifetime) being for the majority the only reality.

> The Nature of Visionary Fancy, or Imagination, is very little Known, & the Eternal nature & permanence of its ever Existent Images is consider'd as less permanent than the things of Vegetative & Generative Nature; yet the Oak dies as well as the Lettuce, but Its Eternal Image & Individuality never dies, but renews by its seed; just so the Imaginative Image returns by the seed of Contemplative Thought.
>
> (K605)

Not that, for Blake, this stupendous archetype is unconnected with history: history, on the contrary, is a mirror in which the realities of the Imagination are continually reflected. So is the life of every individual, and for Blake the Last Judgement is an experience through which individuals, no less than civilizations, must pass, and he himself claimed to have experienced this transforming vision and declared in all simplicity that 'Whenever any Individual Rejects Error & Embraces Truth, a Last Judgement passes upon that Individual'. (K613) However, like so many passages in Blake's writings the simplicity of the words is deceptive, for the spiritual awakening he describes is nothing less than a revelation of 'Truth or Eternity'. Therefore in comparing Blake's Vision of the Last Judgement with that of Michelangelo – to whom Blake was so obviously and so deeply indebted – we are comparing a historical and ecclesiastical with a mystical understanding of the Apocalypse. As we compare the works of these two great Christian artists, each totally dedicated to the religion they professed, we discover that the many differences of overall conception and of detail do correspond to differences in each 'according to the situation he holds'. Indeed it would not be fanciful to surmise that when he wrote this passage, at the beginning of his long and detailed description of his own composition, Blake had in mind differences between his own vision and that of the great Michelangelo whose work he had so long and lovingly studied.

For master to Blake Michelangelo was. Art historians have written on Blake's many debts to Michelangelo; whose work, of course, he knew only in reproduction. Blake was a humble engraver who never visited Italy, though Florentine art was for him supreme. Like Michelangelo's, Blake's art is based on the human figure, and his own Last Judgement, like Michelangelo's, is a composition of human figures. Blake played a great part in introducing the nude figure into English painting, revealing, in Blake's own words, 'naked beauty display'd'. His treatment of the human form has been described as Michelangelesque contours without bulk; whereas Michelangelo's painted figures aspire to the bulk of statues, Blake's forms are linear and weightless versions of the Master's three-dimensional conceptions. It would be easy to say—and art historians are ready to take this view—that Blake merely lacked the skill to give to his linear forms the bodily, earthly bulk of nature. But this is only partially true, for to Blake 'the true man' is not body but spirit. He depicted 'spiritual forms' of intent, considering the corporeal body as only the 'garment' of the soul. In this he follows another Master, Swedenborg, whose presence, along with that of Michelangelo, is to be discovered in his composition of the 'Last Judgement'. Swedenborg, following the 'opening' of his spiritual senses, claimed that he was able to perceive in spiritual vision discarnate men and women in the inner worlds, human-formed but not vested in the red clay of flesh and blood. Blake claimed the same visionary power:

> A Spirit and a Vision are not, as the modern philosophy supposes, a cloudy vapour, or a nothing: they are organized and minutely articulated beyond all that the mortal and perishing nature can produce. He who does not imagine in stronger and better lineaments, and in stronger and better light than his perishing and mortal eye can see, does not imagine at all. The painter of this work asserts that all his imaginations appear to him infinitely more perfect and more minutely organized than anything seen by his mortal eye. Spirits are organized men. (K576–7)

No doubt Blake did possess this power of visualising imaginative forms; but he is also writing as a lifelong follower of Swedenborg. His rejection of art which copies from nature follows from, and corresponds with, his view of man as a spiritual being clothed in a perishing and mortal body.

This difference between Michelangelo's Judgement, conceived as history and as taking place in this world, and Blake's conception of the Apocalypse as a vision of the inner worlds accounts for many differences in composition and conception. Blake once wrote in no doubt excessive enthusiasm that Frere's symbolic diagrams illustrating the mystical system of the German alchemist Jacob Boehme were 'greater than Michelangelo'. This, pictorially speaking, is nonsense, but the phrase expresses at once Blake's high regard for Michelangelo – the standard of all comparison – and the respect in which Blake's scale of values differed from that of the great painter and sculptor of the human body: Frere's illustrations to Boehme are diagrammatic depictions of inner worlds. We see therefore in Blake's departures from Michelangelo a change not only in style but in kind. He is moving away from that tradition of Western art which has so grandly and movingly depicted the human body towards a different kind of art, more often found in Eastern than in Western countries, and whose purpose is not to represent nature but invisible inner worlds.

But let us first look at the similarities of these two amazing conceptions. There is no comparison between Blake and Michelangelo in execution – that goes without saying – between the supreme masterpiece of the Sistine Chapel and Blake's two surviving renderings – the second only a pencil drawing – of his vision. The first is a watercolour version made before 1808 for the Countess of Egremont and now in Petworth House, and the second a pencil drawing made a year or two later as a draft of the painting – now lost – on which he continued to work until near the end of his life (he died in 1827). Neither drawing is to be compared, for that matter, with Blake's own finest work, with his best paintings, his luminous watercolours, or with his magnificent engravings illustrating the Book of Job, and some of his unfinished series of illustrations to Dante. (He learned Italian, when over sixty, in order to read Dante in his own language). Yet in greatness of conception the two are comparable.

At first sight Blake's 'Last Judgement' might seem to be a crowded imitation of Michelangelo's. Yet in the very figure of Jesus we can at once begin to discern the differences of purpose between the two artists. At first glance the magnificent figure of Jesus strikes the spectator of Michelangelo's composition. As we look at the resplendent figure of the Christ, it is he, a godlike man, who comes in judgement, his gesture condemning the wicked as he allows the just to ascend; although indeed it is towards the damned that he turns in condemnation rather than to the blessed in welcome. The vision of the Apocalypse was for Michelangelo and for his time rather one of terror and of this world's ruin than of a spiritual resurrection. So it has remained in the imagination of Christendom as a whole, and so perhaps it must be always for this secular world, whose foundations are to be shaken and overthrown. That Michelangelo's figure of Jesus comes rather as a figure of wrath than of serenity clearly reflects Michelangelo's own political bitterness at the state of the Roman See. His sonnet (No. IV) on Rome in the Pontificate of Julius II expresses, indeed, not only a hope but a passionate wish that Jesus might arrive in the guise of the punisher of corruption:

> Here helms and swords are made of chalices:
> The blood of Christ is sold so much the quart:
> His cross and thorns are spears and shields; and short
> Must be the time ere even his patience cease.
>
> (tr. John Addington Symonds)

Michelangelo's vision considers the great event from the standpoint of this world. The central impression of his painting is of the emergence, as it were the unlooked-for arrival of the stern and majestic figure of Jesus Christ on the human scene. Every human figure in his great composition is likewise individualized, (as for Dante, whom both our painters supremely admired) dramatized, one might say. Among the many great figures who represent humanity active on the field of this world's history, his Jesus reigns supreme, by right of pre-eminence, the greatest among the great. Michelangelo's Jesus has been likened to the sun-god, the Greek Apollo, the *sol invictus* of classical mythology as represented in those classical sculptures so greatly admired by Renaissance humanists. Michelangelo's Jesus emerges in action; his aspect is commanding, his gesture commanding as he enters the human scene as the god-man. W. B. Yeats, who was not only William Blake's first editor, but who equally admired Michelangelo, sees in the Adam of the Sistine Chapel the supreme expression of the Western ideal of man in his mortal beauty:

> Michelangelo left a proof
> On the Sistine Chapel roof
> Where but half-awakened Adam
> Can disturb globe-trotting Madam
> Till her bowels are in heat,
> Proof that there's a purpose set
> Before the secret working mind:
> Profane perfection of mankind.
>
> (Under Ben Bulben)

It is this profane perfection that set its seal on Post-Renaissance art. Nor is the beauty of Michelangelo's Jesus different in kind from the beauty of his Adam, or the magnificent sculpture of Lorenzo di Medici, or of the many splendid figures depicted in the 'Last Judgement'. It is an individual man, godlike among his peers, who comes to judge the world in terms of its own attainable perfection. Not so for Blake: the Jesus of his 'Last Judgement' is not even clearly delineated: rather he is the heart of a divine radiance. He is but the figure on the Throne of God. It is by his presence, not by his pre-eminence, that he reigns.

It is true that already in Michelangelo's painting there is a tendency towards the unity of the mandala form, but in Blake this unity is more striking. Within that unity his Jesus is less a supreme ruler than a permeating presence, the heart of that great circulation of human figures ascending and descending in unbroken flow from the heavens down to the hells, and again rising upwards into the heavens. In the later drawing this unity of life, of 'all the innumerable multitudes of eternity'—in Blake's phrase—is even more apparent than in the first, which is closer to Michelangelo. Thus Blake's Jesus is not so much an individual as the heart of the light which emanates from a divine centre. There is, around Michelangelo's Christ, only so much light as serves to dramatize the entry of the god-man; in both Blake's compositions the enthroned figure of Jesus emerges from the light of the heavenly world itself, whose presence He is.

It is not my purpose to make detailed pictorial comparisons for their own sake, and I will only briefly indicate that many could be made, and have been made. In both paintings there are single figures and groups of figures, those on the left falling headlong, those on the right ascending. Many of these are copied by Blake from Michelangelo, and indeed some recur—and these the most dramatic—elsewhere in Blake's work; like the headlong fall of Satan illustrated in the engravings of the Book of Job. Michelangelo's animating skeletons are to be found also in Blake's composition, and again the theme of the living skeleton is one he uses elsewhere, notably in the *Book of Urizen*. Blake's work, however, makes no use of classical symbolism, like the boat of Charon so dramatically introduced into the Sistine Chapel painting. Blake's symbolic figures are with very few exceptions Biblical, and in the infernal cavern reigns not the Classical Hades but the seven-headed Satan of St. John's Apocalypse. Nor did Blake attempt, as did both Dante and Michelangelo, to make his painting a political commentary on his own time by introducing living or recent historical figures. This is the more noteworthy because in earlier works, like his poem *The French Revolution*, Blake had himself done so and his omission of these can hardly, therefore, be an oversight but rather a deliberate decision. Adam and Eve, Cain and Abel, Abraham and Noah are not for Blake historical figures but rather symbolical; for Blake the Bible was much more than a document of ancient history: 'The Hebrew Bible & the Gospel of

Jesus are . . . Eternal Vision or Imagination of All that Exists' (K604) and

> It ought to be understood that the Persons, Moses & Abraham, are not here meant, but the States Signified by those Names, the Individuals being representatives or Visions of those States as they were reveal'd to Mortal Man in the Series of Divine Revelations as they are written in the Bible; these various States I have seen in my Imagination; when distant they appear as One Man, but as you approach they appear Multitudes of Nations. (K607)

The term, together with his conception of 'states' comprising multitudes of individuals under the symbol of some Biblical figure, Blake took from Swedenborg. Michelangelo's treatment of the Last Judgement doubtless has its inspiration in historic events of the time of the Renaissance, and the conflicts of the Reformation. Blake's interest in the theme has quite a different origin: the theme of a Last Judgement was central to the teachings of Swedenborg. Indeed Blake's great composition could be described as an expression of this Swedenborgian teaching, no less truly than Dante can be called a Thomist with strong Augustinian elements, or Michelangelo seen as an expression of the spirit of Savonarola.

For Swedenborg and for Blake a Last Judgement is at once the end of one era and the beginning of a new; it is the destruction of one 'heaven' and 'earth' but at the same time an epiphany of a new heaven and a new earth. Whereas the darkness and destruction of this world prevails in Michelangelo's painting over the promised appearance of Jesus bringing with him a new heaven and a new earth, Blake's 'Last Judgement' depicts very clearly the bright heavens now opened within the inner worlds of humanity. For Blake the theme of the Apocalypse had therefore an altogether special and burning immediacy in his own time and place, and (perhaps because he was himself born in the very year of Swedenborg's prophecy) he felt himself to be a prophet of the New Age, of the divine-humanity of Jesus in the Swedenborgian sense. Whereas to Michelangelo Christ is the god-man or godlike man, to Swedenborg and to Blake Jesus is the universal Christ who appears in 'the heavens' – that is to say the inner worlds – of all mankind.

Swedenborg's greatest visionary conception is of his 'Grand Man of the heavens'; who appears (so he puts it) 'from a distance' to be one man, but from nearer view is seen to be made up of multitudes of blessed spirits. Blake throughout his writings and in his great visual conception of the Last Judgement brings to life this Swedenborgian realization.

Blake indeed goes so far as to denounce the very notion that the Christ can be limited to the single individual, the historic Jesus:

> No Individual ought to appropriate to Himself
> Or to his Emanation any of the Universal Characteristics
> Of David or of Eve, of the Woman or of the Lord. (K736)

Thus in Michelangelo we see the perfection of what Blake calls the 'vegetated Christ', the human individual Yeats's 'profane perfection of mankind'; in Blake the risen Christ enthroned in the 'heavens', the inner worlds of all humankind.

Not only is the Divine Humanity the sum of all the blessed spirits who together comprise the 'heavens' but so with all the 'states' of being, whether of the heavens or of the hells. Within the greater being of the Divine Humanity all these States exist, like organs within a single body. Of all these human States the Scriptures provided Blake (following Swedenborg) with representative types of 'All that can happen to Man in his pilgrimage of seventy years'. (K638) Doubtless Blake had 'seen' them; but he is none the less expressing Swedenborgian doctrine, and what follows has its parallel in any number of passages throughout the writings of Swedenborg describing his 'visions': 'when distant they appear as One Man, but as you approach they appear Multitudes of Nations.' Thus the groups of figures, or individual figures, in Blake's composition are representative of collectivities, the composition as a whole representing the universal body of the Divine Humanity, the Grand Man of the Heavens. So understood the painting's approximation to an organic unity comprising in a single life all the figures, whether in the celestial, the infernal, or the intermediate regions, becomes understandable; as does the appearance of a flow, a circulation of life within the unity – the Person – within whom all humanity is seen to live and move and have our being.

Not only are the States representative of the heavens, the hells and the purgatories which in their totality comprise every possibility of human experience, but they also suggest a progression. Indeed the painting suggests the Buddhist Wheel of Life; and Blake conceives the spiritual universe rather as a living process than as a static order. The States are eternal, but human beings progress from state to state:

> Distinguish therefore States from Individuals in those States.
> States Change, but Individual Identities never change nor cease.
> (K521)

The heavens, the hells, all the possible states of the soul, are ever-present possibilities through which men pass. Blake did not believe that either the heavens or the hells are once-for-all assigned to human souls, but rather that man is a 'mental traveller' who explores all the possible states, all of them (as in the Buddhist mythology) relative or illusory. He writes of 'the Lost Traveller's dream under the hill' – referring, it seems, to Dante's hells under the mountain of Purgatory. But, lost though he be in the hells, the Traveller is not bound to remain in these dark states, and indeed there is precedent in Dante's own journey for Blake's view; which is nevertheless closer to Buddhist than to Christian orthodoxy, not least so in Blake's view that the 'heavens' are themselves transient:

> . . . it will be seen that I do not consider either the Just or the Wicked to be in a Supreme State, but to be every one of

> them States of Sleep which the soul may fall into in its deadly dreams of Good & Evil when it leaves paradise following the Serpent. (K614)

It is from Swedenborg that Blake derived his view of the human souls passing through successive states according to their guiding will and desire, free to move to higher or lower states, irrevocably bound to none. The 'State called Satan' cannot be redeemed, but individuals may be redeemed *from* that state. There is, besides, a 'supreme state', and this is the Divine Humanity, who is, for Blake, the God within.

It might be possible to argue that Michelangelo's composition represents Apostolic Catholic Christianity, Blake's a Protestant and personal vision. Yet I believe this is a less profitable distinction than that between the exoteric and the mystical understanding of the Last Judgement. Blake himself, our greatest English Christian visionary and prophet, never himself went to church; and his vision transcended all sectarian distinctions. He deplored the division of the Church, and writes:

> Remember how Calvin and Luther in fury premature
> Sow'd War and stern division between Papists & Protestants.
> Let it not be so now! (K507)

But for Blake Jesus is something more specific: he is 'Jesus, the Imagination', the 'supreme state' of humanity which transcends, and releases from, all the states of good and evil through which human souls pass. The presence of Jesus the Imagination is with every man at all times present, born with every birth, accompanying every soul throughout life as the 'saviour' who releases the man from his present state. It is Satan, the Selfhood, who identifies the man with his present state; and who therefore is the Accuser who condemns; the Divine Humanity, Jesus the Imagination, is the ever-present way of release from the states. Imagination is called the 'saviour' because the Person of the Divine Humanity is able to

. . . take away the imputation of Sin
By the Creation of States & the deliverance of Individuals
Evermore. Amen.
But many doubted & despair'd & imputed Sin & Righteousness
To Individuals & not to States . . . (K648)

[But] the Imagination is not a State: it is the Human Existence
itself. (K522)

Both the heavens and the hells Blake saw as alike remote from this state, the heavens of the self-righteous condemning in 'cruel holiness' the hells of the sinners; and he goes on to write:

Yet they are blameless, & Iniquity must be imputed only
To the State they are enter'd into, that they may be deliver'd.
Satan is the State of Death & not a Human existence;
But Luvah is named Satan because he has enter'd that State:
A World where Man is by Nature the enemy of Man,
Because the Evil is Created into a State, that Men
May be deliver'd time after time, evermore

– and the passage concludes:

Learn, therefore, O Sisters, to distinguish the Eternal Human
That walks about among the stones of fire in bliss & woe
Alternate, from those States or Worlds in which the Spirit
travels
This is the only means to Forgiveness of Enemies. (K680)

Human beings can be forgiven for they are not irrevocably 'evil' but can pass through many states, and the supreme state is the goal of all. Thus in Blake's great composition the light of Jesus the Imagination reaches to all the figures, alike the righteous who are ascending and the sinners falling, save only the cavern of the seven-headed Satan, who represents the 'state of death'. Blake's own words best describe his vision of 'Jesus the Imagination' as depicted in his Vision of the Last Judgement:

> Around the Throne Heaven is open'd & the Nature of Eternal Things Display'd, All Springing from the Divine Humanity. All beams from him, as he himself has said, All dwells in him. He is the Bread & the Wine; he is the Water of Life. (K612)

Michelangelo has captured the aspect of the terror we associate with the end of the temporal world; Blake has captured the joy of the dawning of the vision of the eternal, of things as they are, seen in the light of the Imagination, Who condemns none.

One further example will serve to illustrate the great difference between Michelangelo's conception of the Apocalypse and William Blake's. Michelangelo's awesome vision extends from the bursting of the graves at the bottom of the picture to the very heavens; for to the right and to the left, as the eye ascends above the figure of Christ, are two panels; and upon these we are shown the instruments of the Passion, the pillar and the scourge, the nails and the spear, and the cross. It is as if Michelangelo (expressing the mind of his age) sees with dramatic clarity the significance of sacred history in this world but stops short at death. Here is no epiphany of the heavens such as Dante had seen before him and Blake was to see after. In Blake's two compositions, both the earlier version and the later, above the enthroned figure of Jesus the heavens open. On the left and the right of the figure of Jesus are a font, in which an infant is being baptized; and an altar with the bread and the wine, the sacraments by which humankind enters heaven. Directly above the enthroned Divine Humanity is a depiction of the Ark of God. In the first version, Blake, like Michelangelo, has exalted the Cross into the heavens; he describes this first version as follows:

> Behind the Seat & throne of Christ appears the Tabernacle with its Veil opened: the Candlestick on the right: the Table with Shew Bread, on the left: & in the midst, the Cross in

> place of the Ark, with the two Cherubim bowing over it. (K444)

Elsewhere Blake has written that

> Man is the ark of God; the mercy seat is above, upon the ark; cherubims guard it on either side, & in the midst is the holy law; man is either the ark of God or a phantom of the earth & of the water. (K82)

Here instead of the Holy Law we find the Cross; but the cross has become a cross of light, signifying the redemption from the law.

In the later composition an interesting change has been made. Again I quote Blake's own description:

> Over the Head of the Saviour & Redeemer The Holy Spirit, like a Dove, is surrounded by a blue Heaven in which are the two Cherubim that bow'd over the Ark, for here the temple is open'd in Heaven & the Ark of the Covenant is as a Dove of Peace. The Curtains are drawn apart, Christ having rent the Veil. The Candlestick & the Table of Shew-bread appear on Each side; a Glorification of Angels with Harps surround the Dove. (K613)

Blake goes on to describe the Mount of God from which flows the River of Life on whose banks grows the Tree of Life among whose branches temples and pinnacles, tents and pavilions, gardens and groves, display Paradise with its inhabitants.

The Cross, in this second composition, is not exalted into heaven. It is falling, enwrapped by the Serpent, down into the Abyss among the falling figures on the left of the composition. What led Blake to make this significant change between the first and the second versions? It was surely not merely in imitation of Michelangelo that in the first version he exalts the Cross. Blake's Christianity, like Michelangelo's, was deep and lifelong. But it is as if a truth had come to him, as he considered his theme—or contemplated his 'vision'—that the Cross belongs in its nature to this world, not to the highest heavens. There is no Cross in the new heaven and the new earth opened behind the figure of Christ Enthroned. These belong to the 'former days' which have passed away.

In the earlier composition it is not the Cross that is enwound by the Serpent and falling headlong, but Satan. Blake's description is as follows: 'beneath Moses & from the Tables of Stone which utter lightnings, is seen Satan wound round by the Serpent & falling headlong'. (K443) In the second version it is the Cross that is enwound by the Serpent and falling headlong.

In a late poem, *The Everlasting Gospel*—which is in fact a concise statement of Swedenborg's essential teachings—there is a passage that combines the images of Satan and the Cross and the Serpent in a striking manner. According to Swedenborg Jesus was not born free from the sinfulness of human nature but overcame sin in his life, and finally on the Cross:

> He scourg'd the Merchant Canaanite
> From out the Temple of his Mind,
> And in his Body tight does bind
> Satan & all his Hellish Crew;
> And thus with wrath he did subdue
> The Serpent Bulk of Nature's dross
> Till he had nail'd it to the Cross.
> . . .
> He took on Sin in the Virgin's Womb,
> And put it off on the Cross & Tomb (K749)

These lines clarify the symbolic transition from Satan falling headlong entwined by the Serpent in the first version to the Cross entwined by the Serpent in the second. But the passage concludes with the unexpected line, Jesus overcame his own 'Satan' on the Cross 'To be Worship'd by the Church of Rome.'

Now Blake was not at all anti-Papist, rather the contrary, for he admired the Roman Church as a theocracy, declaring that he considered the subjects of the Pope as 'the happiest on earth'. He bitterly compared the enlightened patronage of art by the Papacy — thinking, no doubt, again, of Michelangelo specifically — with the vulgar commercialism of his own time and place. He also praised the Roman Church because it teaches the forgiveness of sins; contrasting this with the censorious Deism of his own time and place. But in the exaltation of the Cross — and this became exaggerated both in Reformation Protestantism and Counter-Reformation Catholicism — Blake saw a failure to see the Risen Christ beyond the Cross. Yet I wonder — and here I am speculating — whether his castigation of the Church of Rome in this context is not inspired only by general considerations but by long contemplation of Michelangelo's 'Last Judgement', in which the Cross and the other instruments of the Passion, and not the vision of the new heaven and the new earth described by St. John in his Apocalypse, is exalted into the highest place in the great painting, where according to Blake's vision, heaven itself should be? Is his castigation a specific criticism of the painting in the Sistine chapel rather than a generalization?

Thus whereas for Michelangelo the Last Judgement represents the end and downfall of the world, for Blake it represents rather an opening of the eyes of the spirit, an end only of illusion to make way for a vision of eternal reality.

Michelangelo's Jesus is a man, Blake's Jesus is Man, as he was created in the image and likeness of God, according to the first chapter of the book of Genesis, the Word, who according to the first chapter of the Gospel of St. John, was with God in the beginning, 'the light that lighteneth every man that cometh into the world'. Such is the Divine Humanity whose theophany Blake announced in his writings, and saw continually in a vision of whose splendour the two drawings that survive give only a faint conception.

The Sleep of Albion

THERE IS, in the treasury of every nation, a body of mythology, legend and folklore, interwoven with history and prehistory, associated with certain places and the names of kings and heroes, with events natural and supernatural, preserved by tradition both oral and recorded. These legends and records belong to the whole people, lending to each brief, unremarkable life a larger identity and participation, as if in some sense these stories were our own. They give us a place in history—and not merely in history but in a story whose imaginative meaning goes beyond history, lending a sense of glory and cosmic significance, and a beauty special to our own people and place on earth. Therefore, we are considering a mass of material which, although it may have its basis in actual events, in real men and women who lived and loved and battled and quested, and who may very well be buried in the sites associated with them, eludes the kind of factual proof or disproof nowadays so popular with the excavators and researchers, all the error-proof techniques which modern fact-finding demands. That the stories have been told and re-told is the only certain fact about them.

Such is what is known as the 'Matter of Britain', the corpus of British history and prehistory, as it has been handed down, and so designated in distinction from the 'Matter of Rome', established in the legends of the founding of the city by Romulus and Remus, fostered by the she-wolf, fit nurse of Rome's military genius; and the story of the conquest of Aeneas, refugee from Troy. France's 'matter' centres round Charlemagne and his knights; and the Teutonic nations likewise have their legendary history interwoven with myth and miracle—all those themes of Odin and Asgard, Siegfried and Parsifal that Wagner has recreated in his opera.

The Matter of Britain too traces our origin back to Troy through the legendary Brut, who is said to have founded his kingdom in these isles; but also has roots in the prehistory and myths of the most ancient indigenous Celtic peoples, a marvellous mingling of Christian and pre-Christian themes. Above all the Matter of Britain centres about a fifth-century Romanized British king or warleader, King Arthur, his chivalry, his court at Camelot, his round table, and the mysterious sanctity, neither wholly Christian nor wholly pagan, of the Holy Grail and its Quest. Doubtless there was a historical personage, a leader of cavalry as introduced and used by the Romans, at a time when the Saxon invaders fought on foot. Perhaps there was a Battle of Badon Hill in which the Saxons on foot were routed by a smaller number of mounted cavalry. There may even have been a Round Table, whether at Glastonbury or elsewhere, long turned to dust. But Arthur, the 'once and future king' of Britain is far greater than any historical personage who may once have borne that name. Indeed the disentangling of the basis of historical fact from the whole tradition and literature of Arthur, his knights and his round table, would be an exercise in reductionism which could serve only to make him less 'real' as a presence, an archetype of kingship within the national imagination of the British people.

Rather than what remains when legend has been stripped away, King Arthur is the sum of all that has been recorded and imagined, written, told, sung and believed. He is a creation of, and a presence in, the national imagination, which has from century to century—even to the present day—continued to adorn Arthur and his court with all those attributes we would most wish to find in the person and circumstances of the perfect king. Arthur embodies the virtues of justice, fortitude, prudence and magnanimity as the British have conceived them; he commands the loyalty of knights of prowess, and establishes peace in his regions. Arthur's court, moving from place to place, confers its half-rustic splendour on these places where its joyous contests in arms and festivals shed a kind of beauty still somehow recognizably and specifically English, where good manners go hand in hand with good cheer. The Arthurian cycle, for all the confusion and treachery of the king's overthrow by his nephew or son Mordred is a joyous one, not tragic like the story of Roland, nor bloodthirsty like the barbaric heroic Irish epic of Cuchulain and Queen Maeve. There is something of Shakespeare's Forest of Arden about Arthur's court. As for the 'round table' there are scholars who associate it with Near-Eastern legends of the King of the World whose Round Table is the zodiac and signifies spiritual world-rulership. Arthur's association with the constellation Arcturus, the Great Bear, casts his image as far as the stars, those enduring records of human dreams. There is something humane, pleasant, something of the English countryside in early summer (he held his court at the Feast of Whitsuntide) in Arthur's civilized yet rural kingdom. The British imagination has, in Arthur's kingdom of peace and justice, from Malory to Tennyson to the present day perfected an image of a ruler finely balanced between strength and mildness; an epitome, one might say, of the image of kingship latent in every Englishman.

The Matter of Britain remains very much alive in this country; one may cite John Cowper Powys's strange fantasy novel, *Porius*; T. E. White's *The Sword in the Stone* and its continuation in *The Once and Future King*; John Heath Stubbs's *Artorius* which some years ago won the Queen's Medal for poetry; and a recently published *Matter of Britain* by Harold Morland, not to mention the film *Camelot*. Towering among these is David Jones's *The Sleeping Lord*.

But myths and legends do not embody merely high ideals and things as moralists think they should be; the imagination of a race is much richer than that, and more mysterious. Arthur's marriage with Guinevere was flawed by the Queen's love for Launcelot du Lac, and by this knight's divided loyalty. Love, as is usually so in mythological stories, obeys laws of its own: Guinevere with her feminine un-law-abidingness is Queen by right of that very independence of the moral law, which she shares with Ireland's Queen Maeve, and Isolde Queen of Cornwall, and with many a goddess. The Eternal Feminine is above, or beneath, or at all events outside all those laws, however admirable, that kings and law-makers establish. Indeed the figures constellated about Arthur are scarcely less potent than the King himself—Gawain and Perceval and the other knights of the Grail quest; and Merlin the magician, type of the magical knowledge of the pre-Christian world, educator and adviser of the King. Merlin too is outside human law and order, reminding that human rule is only relative and itself comprehended within a mystery which the magician may mediate but which neither he nor any human power can control. That kingship is itself decreed and bestowed by higher powers is implicit in that other familiar Arthurian story of the sword in the stone which could only be withdrawn by the divinely appointed heir to the kingdom.

And finally there is the legend of Arthur's death-sleep, somewhere in a secret cave where, with his knights around him, he awaits the time when he will return to restore just rule to his kingdom and to repel its enemies. It is above all this tradition of the sleeper who will wake at the time of need which lives on in the English imagination. Those who remember the Second World War remember how this myth was 'in the air' and cast its glamour on our great war leader Winston Churchill. Indeed this legend is never far below the surface in the national imagination; it is whispered that this or that royal prince may be Arthur returned to restore the kingdom to its golden age. Do people really believe this? Belief is probably the wrong word; not, certainly, as fact, but the archetype is a fact of the imagination and as such very real. Many are the sites in England and Wales that claim to be the king's burial-place. The sword Excalibur is said to have been thrown into Lake Ullswater (once within the boundaries of the British-Welsh kingdom) to summon the Three Queens in their boat. Also told in Northumberland is a story—recently re-told in *The Matter of Britain* by Harold Morland—which sites the cave where Arthur sleeps at Howsteads on Hadrian's Wall from Newcastle to Carlisle. It is said that a shepherd knitting a scarf as he tended his flock dropped his ball of wool, which ran away under the brambles and disappeared. The shepherd followed, and making his way through the tangled thicket came to a cleft in the rock through which he descended into a cave. There he saw the sleeping form of the King, and nearby a table on which was a sword and a horn. The shepherd took up the sword and struck the table. At this the King opened his eyes, and half rose, only to say, 'You should have blown the horn', before falling back into his long sleep.

One recalls other legends of sleepers; there were the Seven Sleepers of Ephesus; the German Barbarossa; the God Saturn himself sleeps in 'the Fortunate Isles'—Great Britain—the God of the Golden Age which was once and will be again. Sometimes the sleeper is a figure of spiritual wisdom—Christian Rosencreuz, who sleeps in the sacred shrine of the Fama Fraternitatis, the Rosicrucians. Always there are the same stories, from the Cheviots to the Catskills, of some simple man who has come unawares upon the sleeper; and never is it certain where he lies. How different from the tomb of Napoleon, or of the Medicis, of Akhbar or of any of the great and illustrious figures of this world! The truly archetypal kings are not to be found in tombs like these, and about them always is an aura of the supernatural.

Both W. B. Yeats and his early friend the Irish mystic, A.E., attached great importance to the sacred sites and holy places of Ireland; to 'marrying', as Yeats put it, the imagination of the people to lake and mountain and rock and river—to the land itself. The Holy Land of Christianity is elsewhere, in the Near-East; for the

Jews the land of Israel is their own land, the place of their ancestors; but for the Christian world Jerusalem and Sinai and Zion and Canaan are in effect—or were until this century for most untravelled human beings—imaginary places. Perhaps the persistence of the Arthurian legends we owe in part to the necessity for holy places in the very land we inhabit. The vision of the house of the Virgin Mary at Walsingham gave rise to England's most famous place of pilgrimage of the late middle ages; a protest, by popular imagination, as it were, against the distancing of sacred sites from our own earth. When the Greeks sent out colonies the colonists would carry with them sacred fire, and would give the name of 'Mount Olympus' (where the Gods live) to the nearest mountain worthy of the name. Blake writes of 'the council of God' meeting on 'Snowdon sublime', the highest peak in Wales and therefore fittest habitation for the spiritual guardians of Britain. This wedding of the imagination of a people to the earth itself serves not only to commemorate historic events and persons but also to give realities of the Imagination (in Shakespeare's words) 'a local habitation and a name'. It does more—it transforms a country, a landscape, into a 'holy land', giving to mountains and rivers and springs and forests a dimension of the sacred—or shall we say, to put it at its lowest, a dimension of poetry?

Seen in this light some may regret that Milton abandoned his first intent of writing his great epic poem on the theme of King Arthur and chose instead *Paradise Lost*, imaginatively situated in regions remote from earth. Poetry cannot fulfil its task of giving to 'airy nothing a local habitation and a name' if the poet chooses to make theology his theme and all his characters save two disembodied spirits. Blake in his Prophetic Books makes London into what Henry Corbin calls an 'emblematic city'. Italy, France and other Catholic countries have succeeded to some extent in localizing the Christian mysteries in their own towns and villages through painting and architecture, but in iconoclastic Protestant countries this has long ceased to be so; and since the Reformation Arthur and his Round Table, Merlin and the Holy Grail have remained our sole national heritage comparable with, for example, the *Ramayana* or the *Mahabharata* in India where real princes and charioteers merge with the world of the gods without losing their roots in history. The forests of Broceliande and of Brindavan are still real forests, to which the names of Merlin and Vivian, of the Lord Krishna and the Gopis, impart a mystery, a sacredness to the real forests of Brittany and of Northern India. When I saw in Delhi a wall said to have been built by the Pandavas, I had the awesome sense of myself entering the realm of myth.

I have long been struck by the fact that while the English and the Germanic nations have superficially so much in common there are deep differences in the archetypal figures that move under the surface, conditioning national character and national history. The figure of Faust, it is true, was the subject of Marlowe's play before Goethe gave to Faust and Mephistopheles that vitality Milton gave to Satan; but it is German writers and psychologists who are forever composing variations on the theme of the pursuit of profane or forbidden knowledge. This restless activity of the godless mind of the human ego symbolized by Faust seems native and congenial to the German genius but has never in the same way (Marlow notwithstanding) 'taken on' in England. It seems that our determining national archetype is that of the Sleeping King. It is not the pursuit of forbidden knowledge but the tendency (like the dormouse in *Alice in Wonderland*) to fall asleep that besets the English. Perhaps Faust will one day be saved; and one day the Sleeper of the ancient British kingdom will awaken. It is such themes as these which have been woven about the British King whose legends have been preserved chiefly in Wales, custodian of the most ancient cultural deposits of the Celtic race which formerly occupied large areas of Great Britain.

William Blake, who called himself 'English Blake', emulated Milton in attempting a national epic, on the theme not of history but of the spiritual destiny of the English nation, in the group of so-called Prophetic Books of which one is entitled *Milton* and the last and most comprehensive, *Jerusalem*. Long incomprehensible because of their unfamiliar mythology whose action takes place not in history but in the inner worlds, Blake's mythological epics are none the less firmly rooted in national events—far more so than is *Paradise Lost*. The unfamiliar supernatural figures are those 'gods' or archetypal energies Blake discerned within the national collective life; and the central figure, whose inner drama is the theme of the whole action, is 'the Giant Albion', the collective person, so to speak, of the nation. Within his 'giant' body are comprehended all the cities and villages and mountains and regions of the British Isles, a national being of the many-in-one and one-in-many. And—perhaps this is not so much strange as inevitable—Blake, for all his admiration for Milton and his Christian faith, has reverted to the national myth of the Sleeping King. Albion is the sleeping 'giant' (not a king, for the 'giant' is not one man but a nation) for whose re-awakening the 'four Zoas' and the other persons of the myth, labour. The Four Zoas are themselves extremely modern 'gods', corresponding as they do to the psychic functions of reason, feeling, sensation and intuition—but even these, as we shall see, have their roots in the 'Matter of Britain' as Blake knew it.

Blake was versed in the Arthurian literature and traditions and it is plain that the Sleeping Arthur is the model of the majestic sleeping form of the Giant Albion. Indeed among Blake's paintings exhibited in his exhibition in 1809 is one entitled *The Ancient Britons* which in his catalogue he describes at length:

> In the last Battle of King Arthur only Three Britons escaped; these were the Strongest Man, the Beautifullest Man, and the Ugliest Man, these three marched through the field unsubdued, as Gods, and the Sun of Britain set, but shall arise again with tenfold splendor when Arthur shall awake from sleep, and resume dominion over earth and ocean. (K577)

There is no question but Blake's Albion is imagined in the similitude of Arthur; for in the same description Blake goes on to write:

> The British Antiquities are now in the artist's hands; all his visionary contemplations, relating to his own country and its ancient glory, when it was, as it again shall be, the source of learning and inspiration. Arthur was a name for the constellation Arcturus, or Boötes, the keeper of the North Pole. And all the fables of Arthur and his round table; of the warlike naked Britons; of Merlin; of Arthur's conquest of the whole world; of his death, or sleep, and promise to return again; of the Druid monuments or temples; of the pavement of Watling-street; of London stone; of the caverns in Cornwall, Wales, Derbyshire and Scotland; of the Giants of Ireland and Britain; of the elemental beings called by us by the general name of fairies; and of these three who escaped, namely Beauty, Strength, and Ugliness. (K577–8)

Thus at the time when he was already at work on his last Prophetic Book, *Jerusalem*, whose plot, so to say, is the sleep and awaking of Albion, the whole Arthurian 'matter' was uppermost in his mind. He goes on:

> The Giant Albion, was Patriarch of the Atlantic; he is the Atlas of the Greeks, one of those the Greeks called Titans. The stories of Arthur are the acts of Albion, applied to a Prince of the fifth century, who conquered Europe, and held the Empire of the world in the dark age, which the Romans never again recovered. (K578)

To the historian it might seem that Blake is here putting things the wrong way round because the historical Arthur is 'real' and the Giant Albion 'imaginary'. But Blake was neither ignorant of history nor simple-minded; as he understood the matter the Giant Albion has the enduring reality of the collective identity and continuing life of the soul of the nation; whereas Arthur was only one individual in whom that soul once expressed itself and around whom the enduring reality of the national life crystallized, so to say. For Blake the Imagination is by no means 'imaginary'; a truth forcefully brought home to us in this century by the psychologists, and especially by C. G. Jung who himself wrote of the 'transpersonal' or 'collective' mind which is shared by some family, tribe or nation, and is, finally, shared by the whole human race. Henry Corbin the Ismaili scholar and metaphysician (and a founding member, with Jung, of the Eranos circle) employed the term 'imaginal' to avoid any ambiguity in the word 'imaginary' with its popular implication of something unreal. On the contrary, all these believed – and Yeats too stated his own belief (in *A Vision*) in the 'angels' who preside over nations – the archetypes of the Imaginal world are human reality itself, the stamp or imprint of human nature in us all. Therefore Blake, in seeing 'the Giant Albion' as the greater and more enduring reality, of whom Arthur was an embodiment and agent, about whose name the idea and ideal of English kingship gathered, is taking the deeper and truer view. The reductionist methods of those who sift out the few grains of material fact (which can of course be found in any body of myth and legend) will have lost the reality of that which they set out to discover somewhere along the way. The Holy Grail is not some Bronze Age cooking pot in a museum, not a gold or silver chalice in church or shrine, but a vision that inspired the imagination of many at a certain period of history; and which continues to do so to this day. Wagner's Parsifal is no less living than the Perceval of the *Mabinogion*. Nor can the kingship of Arthur be dated: it is timeless in the Imagination of the race. These legendary 'deposits' (to use a favourite word of their most recent bard, David Jones) are sacred stories of the British nation. Blake wrote:

> The antiquities of every Nation under Heaven, is no less sacred than that of the Jews. They are the same thing, as Jacob Bryant and all antiquaries have proved. How other

> antiquities came to be neglected and disbelieved, while those of the Jews are collected and arranged, is an enquiry worthy both of the Antiquarian and the Divine. All had originally one language and one religion: this was the religion of Jesus, the Everlasting Gospel. (K578–9)

Thus Blake in recounting 'the acts of Albion' considered himself to be recounting the sacred history – the inner history of the British nation from ancient times, with prophetic foresight of that future when Albion, like Arthur, is to wake from sleep. For all his great admiration for Milton – who himself becomes one of Blake's mythological persons – he himself departs from his model precisely in re-situating sacred history in England's green and pleasant land.

In his poem *Milton* Blake includes one of those passages which have so bewildered readers of a literal-minded kind in its combination of real places with mythological persons and events. So we see Albion

> . . . on his Couch
> Of dread repose seen by the visionary eye: his face is toward
> The east, toward Jerusalem's Gates; groaning he sat above
> His rocks. London & Bath & Legions & Edinburgh
> Are the four pillars of his Throne; his left foot near London
> Covers the shades of Tyburn; his instep from Windsor
> To Primrose Hill stretching to Highgate & Holloway.
> London is between his knees, its basements fourfold;
> His right foot stretches to the sea on Dover cliffs, his heel
> On Canterbury's ruins; his right hand covers lofty Wales,
> His left Scotland; his bosom girt with gold involves
> York, Edinburgh, Durham & Carlisle, & on the front
> Bath, Oxford, Cambridge, Norwich; his right elbow
> Leans on the Rocks of Erin's Land, Ireland, ancient nation.
> (K531)

Thus England's Sleeping Lord covers all the island and includes in his giant body all its inhabitants.

There are many places in the British Isles which claim the tomb of the sleeping Arthur; for Blake's Giant Albion the whole island is his tomb, the 'rock' of Britain in the Atlantic Ocean washed by 'the Sea of time and space.'

> Albion upon the Rock of Ages,
> Deadly pale outstretch'd and snowy cold, storm cover'd,
> A Giant form of perfect beauty outstretch'd on the rock
> In solemn death. (K497)

Sometimes the tomb is called 'the Sick Couch', for Albion's 'death' is a spiritual malady, not a state of non-existence. Blake names the poet Milton 'the awakener', for it is the poets who speak to the nation with the voice of the Imagination.

> Albion's sleeping Humanity began to turn upon his Couch,
> Feeling the electric flame of Milton's awful precipitate descent.
> (K502)

Blake himself was an Awakener at a time he saw as the beginning of a New Age—as witnessed by the American and French Revolutions; England, as always, was slow to respond:

> Awake, thou Sleeper on the Rock of Eternity! Albion awake!
> The trumpet of Judgment hath twice sounded: all Nations are awake,
> But thou art still heavy and dull. Awake, Albion Awake!
> (K506)

But Albion's time has not come; he 'turns upon his couch' then sinks back 'in dismal dreams/Unawaken'd.'

The sleep of Arthur has not in itself any positive significance, and is but the passing of time until the need of his nation summons him to return. But the 'sleep' of the Giant Albion is conceived by Blake not as the mere passage of time but as a state of apathy, of lowering of consciousness, of forgetfulness of higher things. Blake's theme of the sleep and awakening of the soul of the nation embraces far more than the mere return of the Once and Future King at the hour of need: Blake tells the story of how the nation has come to lapse into spiritual ignorance and forgetfulness, of the 'deadly dreams' of the deluded nation—all the cruelties of war and the injustices of peace that result from this alienation—and how the final awakening may come about not at the mere blowing of a horn but through the spiritual labours of the 'awakeners'.

This is not the occasion for describing the involved mythological happenings of the Giant Albion's long 'dream' in the course of the 'deadly sleep' of his wanderings from eternal life. Blake's first version of the theme—*Vala or the Four Zoas*, announces the theme as Albion's

> fall into Division & his Resurrection to Unity:
> His fall into the Generation of decay & death, & his
> Regeneration by the Resurrection from the dead. (K264)

His last Prophetic Book, *Jerusalem*, he introduces in a similar way:

> Of the Sleep of Ulro! and of the passage through
> Eternal Death! and of the awaking to Eternal Life.
> (K622)

For Blake the 'Fall' is not, as for Milton, a fall into sin through disobedience, but a fall into 'sleep' through a closing of consciousness and loss of the 'divine vision':

> Refusing to behold the Divine Image which all behold
> And live thereby, he is sunk down into a deadly sleep.
> (K272)

The 'divine image' is the archetype of human nature imprinted in every soul, as described in the first chapter of Genesis.

But Blake nowhere writes of the 'Fall' in terms of Christian theology (as Milton does) through man's disobedience and sin;

rather he adopts the Platonic view of the human condition as one of forgetfulness of eternal things. All know Plato's myth, (in the Tenth Book of the *Republic*) of the souls who, as they approach generation, reach a river – the river of forgetfulness, where all must drink. Some drink deeply and their forgetfulness of eternity is complete. Others, who wisely refrain from drinking so deeply, retain some memory of eternal things. These are the philosophers, the lovers and the musical souls. For Blake held Plato's view that the soul knows everything, and needs only to remember what it already and for ever knows.

But Albion's 'deadly sleep' is a dire reality of national life, troubled with 'dreams'. It is a state of illusion, a loss of the 'divine vision' in which the nation falls under the power of 'the mind of the natural frame', of the empirical ego. Blake is quite specific in his diagnosis of England's national disease: it is precisely that secular materialism (which Blake associated with the honoured names of Bacon, Newton and Locke) upon which modern Western civilization is founded; and has foundered, some would now say, Blake's prophetic vision having proved truer than his contemporaries could have foreseen. When natural reason usurps the place of imaginative vision and announces 'Now I am God from eternity to eternity', and the 'divine vision' innate in every soul fades from consciousness, the rest follows. This *hubris* of natural reason in its pursuit of natural knowledge outside the context of spiritual wisdom has brought consequences which may well appal us. This Blake had understood at a time when triumphalist mechanistic science was still in its infancy. Again, readers of Blake are shocked when from the charmed regions of mythology we are suddenly jolted into awareness that Blake is talking about realities – ideologies – well known to us and propounded daily on the media with all the assurance of received majority opinion. The 'mind of the natural frame', Urizen – Satan as he is named in the later Prophetic Books – is called 'Newton's Pantocrator, weaving the woof of

Locke'. He is opaque to spiritual knowledge, recognizing only natural fact, and is the very spirit of modern reductionism.

Before this externalization of nature the universe was one with humanity. In his address 'To the Jews' with which Blake introduces the Second Book of *Jerusalem* Blake again alludes to the one universal tradition, claiming that Britain was the original seat of that 'Everlasting Gospel':

> Jerusalem the Emanation of the Giant Albion! Can it be? Is it a Truth that the Learned have explored? Was Britain the Primitive Seat of the Patriarchal Religion? If it was true . . . Ye are united, O ye Inhabitants of Earth, in One Religion, The Religion of Jesus, the most Ancient, Eternal & the Everlasting Gospel . . . 'All things Begin & End in Albion's Ancient Druid Rocky Shore.' (K649)

Blake then goes on to declare that the Hebrew patriarchs learned from 'the Druids', who were priests of this universal religion, and he equates the Adam Kadmon of the Jewish mystical tradition with the Giant Albion; the two symbols having the same significance of the primordial universal humanity:

> You have a tradition, that Man anciently contained in his mighty limbs all things in Heaven & Earth; this you received from the Druids.
>
> 'But now the Starry Heavens are fled from the mighty limbs of Albion'. (K649)

This externalization of the natural universe is illustrated in Plate 25 of *Jerusalem* where Albion is depicted with sun, moon and stars in his 'mighty limbs' from which they are being separated by females representing the agents of natural generation. Can it be that Albion is stirring in his 'sleep' of materialist oblivion? Blake prayed to the divine Spirit for inspiration,

> That I may awake Albion from his long & cold repose;

> For Bacon & Newton, sheath'd in dismal steel, their terrors
> hang
> Like iron scourges over Albion (K635)

– and he indicts the 'schools and universities of Europe':

> And there behold the Loom of Locke, whose Woof rages dire,
> Wash'd by the Water-wheels of Newton; black the cloth
> In heavy wreathes folds over every Nation: cruel Works
> Of many Wheels I view, wheel without wheel, with cogs
> tyrannic
> Moving by compulsion each other, not as those in Eden, which,
> Wheel within Wheel, in freedom revolve in harmony & peace.
> (K636)

Let us not forget that Blake's phrase, the 'dark Satanic mills' refers not to the landscape of the Industrial Revolution but to the mechanistic ideology which created that landscape. Here he contrasts the mechanized wheels of industry with the 'wheel in the midst of a wheel' of Ezekiel's vision of the 'living creatures'. He would see the same black cloth coming from the looms of the Universities to this day and not only those of Europe.

Albion's state of 'eternal death' therefore is seen not in terms of some comfortably remote myth but clearly and precisely identified as the materialist ideology to which the West has succumbed.

There is of course only one sleeping King Arthur; but Blake writes of many 'sleepers' who are the individual lives within the national being; and here again he is close to Plato and Plotinus, who are concerned with individual souls, who as they descend into generation lose their consciousness of eternal things and become 'sleepers'. Plotinus writes of those who transmigrate from one incarnation to another, passing 'as it were from bed to bed, from sleep to sleep'; and Blake too writes of these 'sleepers' who enter the world of generation, whom he calls 'the spectres of the dead'.

He describes in *Milton* in terms rather Platonic than Christian, how the souls 'descend' into this world,

> . . . being piteous Passions & Desires
> With neither lineament nor form, but like to wat'ry clouds
> The Passions & Desires descend upon the hungry winds,
> For such alone Sleepers remain, meer passion & appetite.
> (K512)

Blake describes how Milton himself, for Blake the supreme poet, whom he calls 'the awakener', takes on a human body and thereby enters the state of 'sleep'. But in his sleep he is fed by the angels with 'food of Eden', visions of eternal things:

> As when a man dreams he reflects not that his body sleeps,
> Else he would wake, so seem'd he entering his Shadow: but
> With him the Spirits of the Seven Angels of the Presence
> Entering, they gave him still perceptions of his Sleeping Body
> Which now arose and walk'd with them in Eden.

Milton's 'real and immortal Self' appeared to 'those who dwell in immortality', Blake writes,

> . . . as One sleeping on a couch
> Of gold, and those in immortality [that is the seven Angels] gave forth their Emanations
> Like Females of sweet beauty to guard round him & to feed
> His lips with food of Eden in his cold and dim repose:
> But to himself he seem'd a wanderer lost in dreary night.
> (K496)

Milton and the other poets and visionaries who still in dreams behold eternity labour to clothe and build houses for the 'spectres of the dead' whose sleep is absolute; until 'a vast family, wondrous in beauty and love' is created on earth. So through the infinite labours of love the dead are awakened to life through recollection of eternal things, depicted in works of art.

What is called for is a change in our consciousness itself, that will make us, like Blake, see 'not with but through the eye' – the rising and setting sun, the clouds, the moon and stars, the tree outside the window.

Our society is for ever thinking in terms of changing outer circumstances; Blake's revolution will come about when we change ourselves. From inner awakening outer changes will follow; for we cannot treat a living and holy earth as we would a lifeless mechanism, nor human beings in whom the divine humanity is manifested in all its myriad forms as the 'mortal worm' born in a night to perish in a night. We have created our nightmare world in the image of our ideologies; but with the awakening of our humanity we will see a different world, and create a different world.

When Albion awakens he will find himself in his lost kingdom, restored to its former glory; for the kingdom is in ourselves. In this awakening it is for the poets, painters and musicians to remind Albion – remind the nation – of those higher things he has forgotten. 'Poetry, Painting & Music, the three Powers in Man of conversing with Paradise, which the flood did not Sweep away.' (K609)

Paradise is not a place but a state of being, the lost kingdom to which the sleepers of Albion must someday awake.

Index